MAKING MODERN JEWELLERY

MAKING MODERN JEWELLERY

SIMPLE
TECHNIQUES
MODERN
MATERIALS

PETER BAGLEY

CASSELL

A CASSELL BOOK

First published in the UK
1992 by Cassell
Villiers House
41/47 Strand
London
WC2N 5JE

Distributed in the United States
by Sterling Publishing Co., Inc.
387 Park Avenue South, New York, NY 10016–8810

Distributed in Australia
by Capricorn Link (Australia) Pty Ltd
P.O. Box 665, Lane Cove, NSW 2066

British Library Cataloguing in Publication Data

Bagley, Peter
  Making modern jewellery.
  I. Title
  739.274

  ISBN 0–304–34132–0

Typeset by Chapterhouse Ltd, The Cloisters, Formby

Printed and bound in Hong Kong by Dah Hua Printing Company.

Contents

Introduction

Modern jewellery, like jewellery throughout history, is created to adorn people and enhance their appearance; it also makes a statement about an individual.

The difference between modern and traditional jewellery lies in the greater range of materials and designs that are nowadays possible and acceptable. Before the twentieth century most jewellery, with the exception of some ethnic varieties, was made from the precious metals of gold, silver or platinum combined with precious stones. Other materials were used mainly as a lower-cost alternative to the real thing.

The exhibition of René Lalique's work at the 1900 Exposition Universelle in Paris marked a significant step in the break with this tradition: his bold use of glass, semi-precious stones and enamel prepared the way for greater flexibility in design and use of materials, a trend that gathered impetus in the 1950s and 1960s with the younger generation's newfound freedom of expression, a freedom that was also expressed in the dress revolution.

Many of the materials used to make jewellery nowadays offer colour, texture and ease of working that was not possible, or acceptable, in the past. This, together with the availability of specialized tools and equipment, has brought the creation of jewellery within the scope of any creative and practical person. With a little care, an amateur can produce very sophisticated and exciting pieces.

Designing and making jewellery, either for one's own use or to offer as gifts or for sale, provides limitless scope for individual expression in form and colour. This book offers encouragement to the beginner by describing techniques and suggesting projects that can be carried out with a minimum of equipment and space. For the sake of clarity each chapter deals with one material, though of course the more interesting pieces of jewellery are often made using a variety of materials and more than one technique. None of the processes described requires exceptional skill, but some care is needed, especially when handling tools and substances, such as toxic chemicals, that can cause injury. It is important to take effective precautions, therefore, to prevent both the operator and anyone in the vicinity being hurt. The diagrams show the approximate size of individual projects but of course these can be scaled up or down to suit individual taste.

Most of the materials used in the projects can be purchased from your local hardware store, model or craft shop or department store. More specialized items such as precious metal, findings and stones are easily purchased from catalogues. Addresses for these suppliers' catalogues are found in craft and hobby journals.

Attention to detail is important in jewellery-making. Jewellery is made to be looked at, so casual or sloppy work can have no place in the designing or making of it. That said, the aim is to enjoy making jewellery – so have fun trying out some of the projects and making your own variations.

At the end of the book are useful **conversion tables** (pages 117–21), a **glossary** of words used in jewellery-making (pages 122–4), and, finally, a select **bibliography** (page 125) to guide your further exploration of the subject.

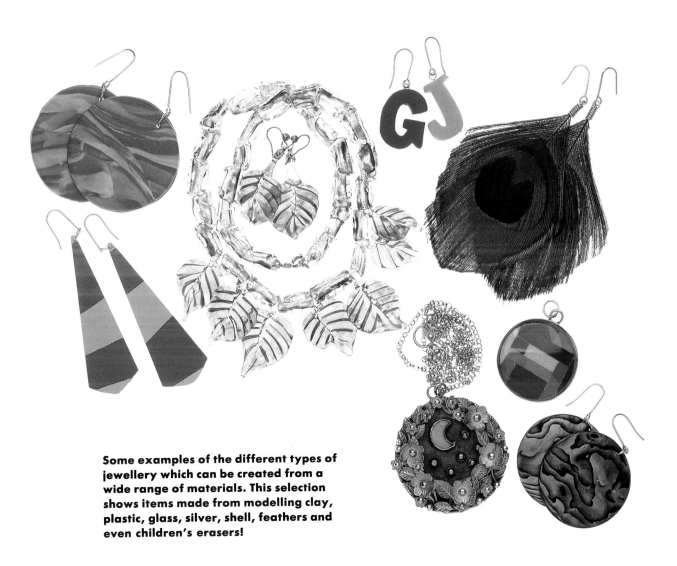

Some examples of the different types of jewellery which can be created from a wide range of materials. This selection shows items made from modelling clay, plastic, glass, silver, shell, feathers and even children's erasers!

1 Design

Good design in jewellery is that magical blend of the concept, material and production method that enhance each other. The shapes, colours and textures you choose will help create a mood – flippant, light-hearted, formal, dominant, free and so on. This is the heart of design. There are no golden rules for good design, only conventions.

The initial idea or concept for a piece can come from a variety of sources: natural forms of flowers, fruit and foliage, mathematical shapes, computer images, buildings and landscape are just some examples. Or it can be simply the quality of the material being used that provides the inspiration.

Then there is the question of how to develop the concept in a suitable way. Material, method of construction, texture, colour: none of these elements can be considered in isolation. You will need to decide how to link your areas or volumes to a backbone (structure), and how to combine and contrast textures and colours to produce an object that is pleasing to look at, practical to wear and economical to produce.

There are a few design conventions, briefly described below, that may guide you in your considerations.

ABSTRACTION

If you plan to make a piece of jewellery based on an existing form you will need to make changes in scale, colour, texture and detail. For example, a flower modelled in metal as an earring may well need to be smaller, and simpler than an actual flower, and its colour and texture will be different. The selection of elements to represent a natural form is known as abstraction. The process can be taken so far that the object is not recognizable as a naturalistic representation (see figs 1 and 2).

SYMMETRY

An essentially simple shape with its reflection can create a more interesting shape with new characteristics. Changing the relationship between reflection and the initial shape can make a more exciting combination (see fig. 4).

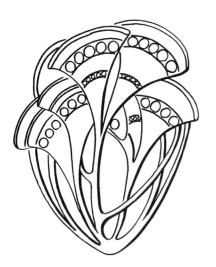

fig. 1
Abstract flower design from an art nouveau brooch by M. Dufrène.

fig. 2
Tolima Pendant of an abstract human figure.

SYMBOLISM

Symbols and signs are conventionally agreed representations of abstract concepts. They play a significant part in jewellery design. For example, you can have a cross to represent Christian ideals, a ring to express the concept of marriage, a heart to represent love (see fig. 3).

BALANCE AND DYNAMICS

Visual balancing of large areas near to the centre of a piece against smaller areas further away, or balancing a large area of pale colour against a small, more intensely coloured one will give a dynamic quality to the piece (fig. 5a). Arrow-shaped or tapered shapes will also give a dynamic quality (fig. 5b).

REPETITION AND PROGRESSION

Repeated shapes create patterns (fig. 6). Varying the size or proportion of a repeated shape can give life and movement to the pattern.

fig. 3
A cross, a heart and a ring are all examples of objects which have a symbolic value (representing Christianity, love and marriage respectively).

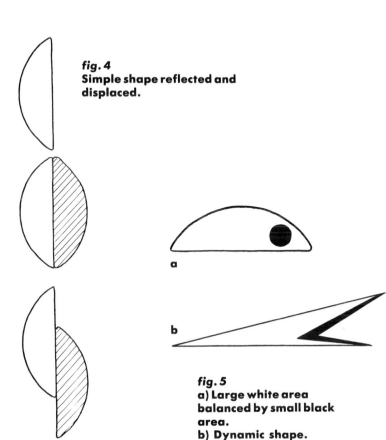

fig. 4
Simple shape reflected and displaced.

a

b

fig. 5
a) Large white area balanced by small black area.
b) Dynamic shape.

fig. 6
Patterns of repeated shapes.

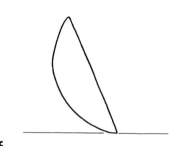

fig. 7
a) **Shape at rest.**
b) **Balanced shape.**
c) **Unstable shape.**

DYNAMICS

Diagonals and arrow shapes convey movement. Gentle curves and straight horizontal lines convey rest (fig. 7).

PROGRESSIVE DIVISION

Dividing an area or a line progressively will lead the eye. For example, a line divided 2:1 repeatedly (fig. 8) leads the eye inwards.

SOFT AND HARD

Simple geometrical shapes, particularly in primary colours, give bold strong statements; by contrast, gentle curves and blended colours give an image of softness (fig. 9).

CONTRAST

Contrasting colour, tone, form, texture and pattern (fig. 10) makes for more interest.

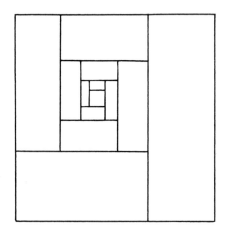

fig. 8
Progressive divisions.

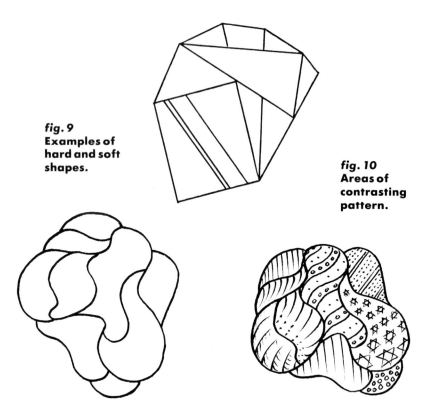

fig. 9
Examples of hard and soft shapes.

fig. 10
Areas of contrasting pattern.

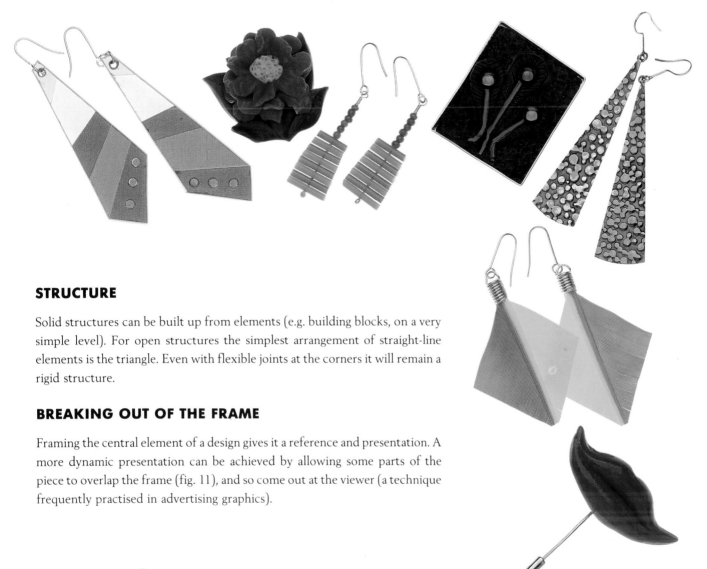

STRUCTURE

Solid structures can be built up from elements (e.g. building blocks, on a very simple level). For open structures the simplest arrangement of straight-line elements is the triangle. Even with flexible joints at the corners it will remain a rigid structure.

BREAKING OUT OF THE FRAME

Framing the central element of a design gives it a reference and presentation. A more dynamic presentation can be achieved by allowing some parts of the piece to overlap the frame (fig. 11), and so come out at the viewer (a technique frequently practised in advertising graphics).

Jewellery designs showing (clockwise from top left) foil mosaic earrings, modelled flower brooch, striped earrings in contrasting colours, modelled brooch with inset glass beads, textured silver earrings, earrings made from cut and dyed feathers, stylized lips stick pin and multi-coloured wood earrings. You can find out more about how to make these items later in the book.

11

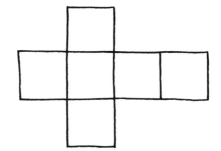

fig. 12
From this flat outline a cube can be formed by folding.

fig. 13
The flat outline for the formation of a three-dimensional pyramid.

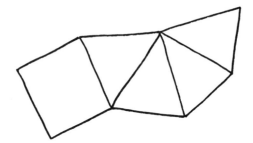

fig. 11
Subject breaking out of the frame.

DEVELOPED SHAPES

Flat shapes can be formed up into three-dimensional solids by folding and curving (figs 12 and 13).

With a malleable material twists and changes of section are possible from a flat shape, as in fig. 14 where flat shapes have been formed up to make a ring.

JOINTS

Pieces of jewellery are typically made from more than one piece of material. The method of joining the various components together is an integral part of the design, the method selected depending on the types of material employed. Many joining techniques form a significant design element. Joining techniques suitable for various materials are dealt with later in the book.

In developing design ideas it is useful first to use pencil and paper, then – often – to make models in the round, using materials such as card, plastic sheet and modelling clay (e.g. Fimo or Plasticine). This is most useful for designs involving three dimensions.

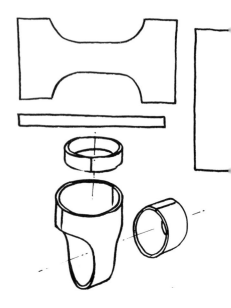

fig. 14
Flat shapes formed up to fabricate a ring.

2 Equipment and Tools

EQUIPMENT

For many amateur jewellers a room that is dedicated solely to the design and production of jewellery is an unattainable ideal: a table in the corner of a room is probably the most they will achieve. But such an arrangement need not inhibit the design and production of high quality and worthwhile work.

A small table can make a suitable **bench**, although the larger and, particularly, the more rigid and heavy it is the better.

fig. 15
Kitchen table adapted for use as a basic work bench showing:
a) bench pin
b) torch rest
c) soldering block
d) anvil post.

fig. 16
Portable
folding work
bench with
clamped on
bench pin.

One very effective arrangement is to clamp a purpose-made top on to a DIY folding work bench (fig. 16). It can be removed and the unit folded away when not required. Alternatively, a home-made or commercial **bench pin** can be clamped to an ordinary table. An important feature of the bench is that it should have a secure mount for a gas torch (used for soldering), so that this can be hooked on to the bench when lit and left there without any danger.

Other basic requirements are a **cutting board** and **anvil**. The cutting board need be no more than a small sheet of hardboard. The anvil can be a small commercial one or almost any heavy lump of steel which will sit firmly and offer a flat working top. It is best to have the anvil supported directly on the floor, e.g. on a raised and substantial wooden post (as in fig. 15), because a bench-mounted anvil will vibrate the contents of the bench unless it is exceptionally rigid.

A **thick sheet of plate glass** or a **plastic pastry board**, is needed for modelling with Fimo, Plasticine and clay.

For anchoring components that are being glued you will find a small **piece of insulation board** (which readily accepts pins) useful.

Silver soldering is usually done on a **charcoal or non-asbestos soldering block**, which can be set on a revolving stand or on fire bricks.

For melting silver or gold for simple casting, an assembly of fire bricks placed to contain the heat but with an air exit at the top of the back wall will prove effective. This is not a technique you will need for any of the projects described in this book.

Good lighting is essential: it is best to have an **adjustable angle lamp** to one side of or at the back of the bench so the light can be directed on the work. When hard soldering it is necessary to judge the temperature of the metal by its colour, which can only be done in a subdued light. So if your bench is near a window you will need some means, such as a window blind, to cut out daylight.

For designing, a **clipboard** and a pack of **cheap typing paper**, together with a selection of **pencils**, **pens**, **eraser** and **coloured pencils** will suffice. A set of **drawing instruments** will prove useful as will **masking tape**, **scissors** and a **pencil sharpener**.

A set of **watercolour** or **gouache paints** is worthwhile if colour is critical at the design stage.

A **multi-drawer unit** for holding findings, stones and components is very useful.

When you are arranging your work place, make sure that you give yourself ready access to your tools. Each should have its place and be instantly to hand when needed.

TOOLS

List 1 on page 17 gives a suggested basic set, useful for making component jewellery, working with most findings, soft plastic, card and other thin non-metal sheet material (see fig. 17).

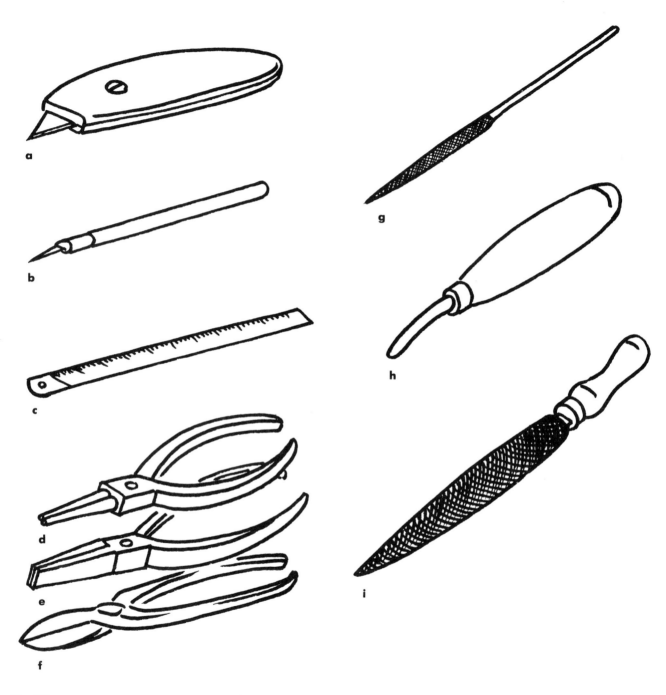

fig. 17
Basic set of tools:
a) large craft knife
b) small craft knife
c) steel straight-edge

d) round-nosed pliers
e) flat-nosed pliers
f) pair of snips

g) half-round Swiss file
h) burnisher
i) half-round file.

LIST 1

Item	Function
Craft knife (large)	cutting non-metal sheet
Craft knife (small)	fine cutting work
Steel straight-edge	cutting straight lines
Round-nosed pliers (smooth jaws)	forming wire
Flat-nosed pliers (smooth jaws)	bending wire and sheet
Pair of snips	cutting sheet metal
Half-round Swiss file	fine shaping of metal
Burnisher	setting stones and foil work
Half-round file, medium (100 mm [4"])	shaping and finishing wood, metal and rigid plastic sheet
Leather punch	making holes in card, leather and plastics
Cutting board	to protect the work top when using craft knife

The addition of tools in List 2 (some of which are shown in fig. 18) will allow the use of precious and base metals, hard plastics and plywood.

LIST 2

Item	Function
Jeweller's saw and blades	cutting intricate shapes in sheet metal
Bench pin	sawing
Small hand-drill and drills	drilling holes
Triblet	for shaping rings
Soldering iron	soft soldering non-precious metal
Scribe	marking out
Dividers	marking out, spacing and scribing circles
Gas torch	hard soldering
Tweezers	hard soldering
Soldering block	hard soldering
Pickle bath and water container	removing flux and scale
Square	setting out lines at 90°, marking right angles
Centre punch	marking holes for drilling
Bench block or anvil	light forging and flattening

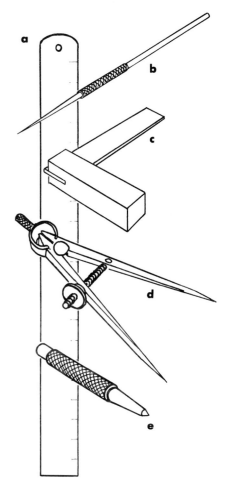

fig. 18
Tools for marking out on metal:
a) steel rule
b) scribe
c) square
d) dividers
e) centre punch.

The addition of tools in List 3 will enable most processes of metal construction to be undertaken.

LIST 3

Item	Function
Rolling mill	rolling sheet and wire thinning
Anvil	forging metal
Buffing machine	mechanical polishing
Pendant drill	drilling holes and shaping with burrs
Bick iron	light forging of bent and folded pieces
Graver	engraving and stone setting
Kiln	enamelling
Lathe	turning wood, metal and plastic
Pillar drill	drilling large holes
Barrelling machine	tumble polishing metal and stones
Dapping block and punches	making metal discs and cutting large holes and making domes

The essential tools required are listed with each project so it is not necessary to rush out at once and buy every tool listed here! Build up your tool collection carefully over a period of time. Keep all cutting tools sharp and all working faces clean and polished.

The consumable materials you will need (e.g. abrasives, polishes, acid pickles) are also listed with each project.

Lastly, a word of warning: be careful with all tools, materials and chemicals, particularly acids. Label all containers holding chemicals and make sure all persons who may have access to them are aware of their dangers. Keep them out of the reach of children.

3 Component Jewellery and Findings

COMPONENT JEWELLERY

A wide range of professional-looking jewellery can be produced using little more than a pair of pliers and some epoxy cement. The components generally require nothing more than simple assembly and the fitting of stones or beads.

Creativity is limited to the selection of the components and stones, but this approach will satisfy many and forms a useful introduction to jewellery making. The metal components are available in base metal with a silver or gilt finish, stainless steel, silver and gold.

Some of the precious metal pieces may require some small amount of metal removal to facilitate the fitting of stones and this is usually accomplished with a half-round Swiss file.

Base metal components have a bright finish that can crack and peel if deformed, so most stones are fitted with an adhesive.

USING COMPONENTS AND CABOCHON STONES

Having selected the stones and components, position them temporarily in their setting to judge the finished effect. Such a dry run will also show up any discrepancies in fit that need to be corrected before adhesive is applied. Some tips: place the stones and components in the lid of a shoe box or similar shallow tray to prevent loss and use a small piece of Plasticine or Blu-Tak for lifting stones into position (see fig. 20). The metal component can be held steady by standing it in a small lump of Plasticine.

Both the surface of the stone and the surface of the component must be dry and free from grease and dirt. A small amount of two-part epoxy resin is squeezed from each tube on to a scrap piece of paper or card and mixed together with a toothpick, cocktail stick, (clean) used match or other disposable piece of wood.

Using the stick, pick up a small amount of the mixed adhesive and spread it on the contact area of the stone. Similarly with the component. Now lift the stone in place and gently push it down to seat it. Enough adhesive should be

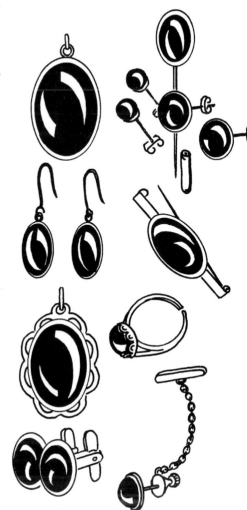

fig. 19
Component jewellery simply set with semi-precious stones.

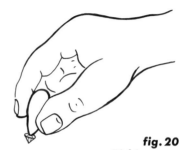

fig. 20
Picking up a small stone with a knob of Plasticine.

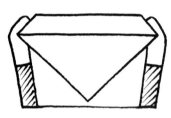

fig. 21
Cross-section of a commercial claw setting for a faceted stone before and after setting.

used to ensure good coverage of the contacting faces but not so much that it oozes out. You should not be able to see the adhesive on the finished piece.

The epoxy adhesive will set more quickly with a little applied warmth. This will be detailed on the maker's instructions. With some settings (plain, lace-edge and mill-edge) the bezel edge can be pushed over, obviating the need for adhesive.

FITTING FACETED STONES

As with cabochon stones, the faceted stone should be placed in the setting to check the fitting. Any unwanted metal must be removed until the stone sits down without rocking. With some settings it is necessary to cut the seating to ensure that the stone sits squarely. When the stone sits well, the claws should project just above the girdle (outside edge) of the stone.

Any final finishing or polishing of the metal component must be done now. Then holding the stone in position with the piece well supported, push one of the claws partly over. Turn the piece around and push an opposite claw over. Repeat the process until the stone is secured all round. The ends of the claws should now be burnished down so that they will not catch.

USING JUMP RINGS

Jump rings have to be opened to thread on the component to be linked. This must be done by *twisting* the ring and not by pulling it open. Use two pairs of pliers or one pair of pliers and a slotted twisting tool to twist the ring open (see fig. 22).

Once you have threaded on the components, the jump ring can be twisted back. (Tip: push the ring very slightly together before twisting and a good closing will result.)

fig. 22
Twisting open a jump ring using two pairs of pliers.

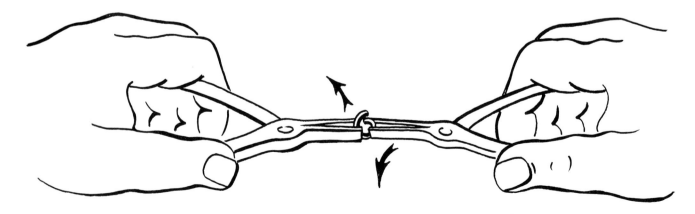

FINDINGS

There are many common elements in jewellery such as catches, pins, ear wires and bolt rings, which can be made but are often more conveniently bought. The following list gives the most commonly used findings.

Bail	shaped open ring for fitting into a cross hole or loop, generally by squeezing
Bead	hollow metal bead
Bell cap	secured to a stone with epoxy adhesive for attaching a jump ring
Bolt ring	open ring with spring closing bolt and attachment loop for fixing on to the end of a neck chain as a fastener. Various qualities are available.
Brooch back	complete brooch pin assembly, generally for fixing by adhesive
Clasp	alternative to a bolt ring for fastening necklaces
Collet	formed metal cup to retain a stone, essentially one of two types: *plain* for mounting cabochon stones, and *claw setting* for mounting faceted stones
Ear wire	for fixing to or suspending an earring piece, available in many forms (hook or butterfly type are most common for pierced ears).
End cup	hollow cup for a decorative termination to a bead necklace
Eye pin	for attaching another component by jump ring, similar to a head pin but terminating in a loop
Head pin	wire with headed end, used to thread beads for pendant earrings
Jump ring	Unjointed wire ring for terminating a chain or linking small components
Liquid silver/gold	tiny metal tubes for threading
Pin	single brooch pin
Pin guard	tubular cap to protect the end of a pin
Ring shank	the part of the ring encircling the finger
Spacer bar	multi-holed bar for spacing strings of beads
Split ring	two-turn ring; an alternative to a jump ring
Stamping	a component produced from sheet metal

In addition to these components, it is possible to purchase complete pieces of jewellery requiring only stones to be fitted.

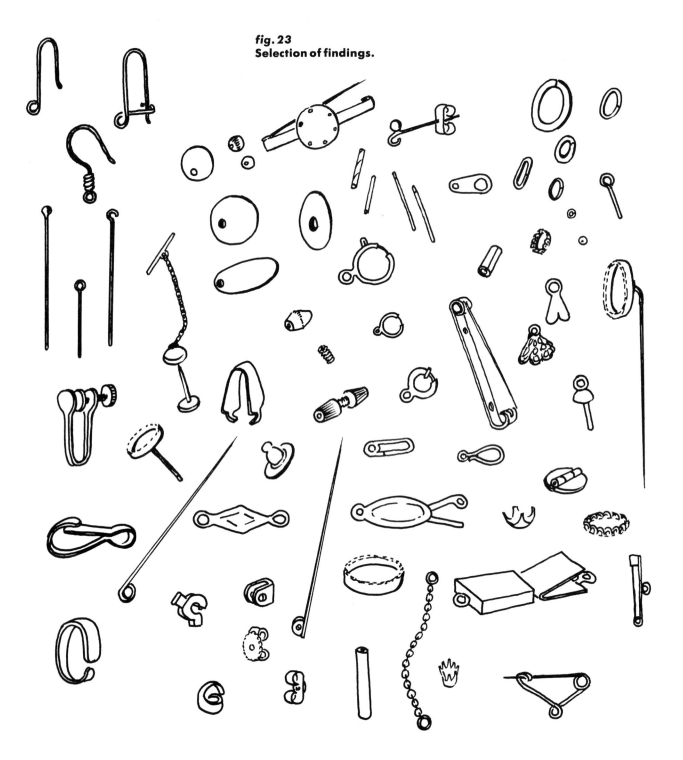

**fig. 23
Selection of findings.**

Selection of findings made from plastic, glass and metal and four different styles of chain – all available commercially.

BEADS

The range of commercially produced beads is enormous and on page 103 you can see just a small selection of available designs. The materials available range from precious or semi-precious stones, pearls and coral to gold, silver and base metals. Wood, clay, plastics and glass are all available in many forms and colours. A good supplier's catalogue is a useful acquisition. Beads are also easy to make in a variety of different styles and shapes and examples of handmade beads are shown below (figs 24–28).

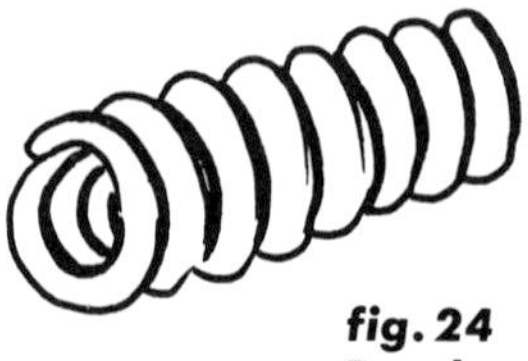

**fig. 24
Bead wound
from round
wire.**

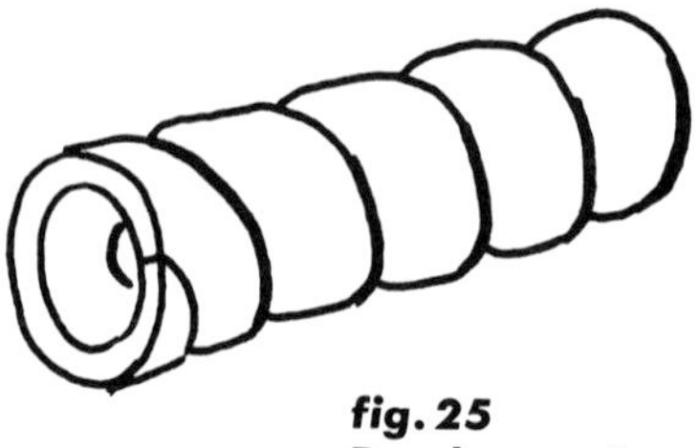

**fig. 25
Bead wound
from flat strip.**

**fig. 26
Molten bead
dropped into
cold water to
form a baroque
shape and then
drilled.**

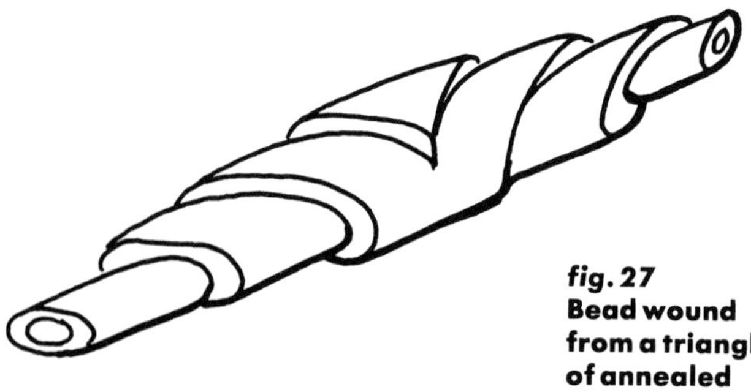

**fig. 27
Bead wound
from a triangle
of annealed
sheet.**

**fig. 28
Melted bead
hammered flat
after cooling
and then
drilled.**

4 Metals: Properties and Methods of Working

Metal is the most common material used for making jewellery and particularly for those parts of jewellery which contact the body such as rings, earring fittings, chains and functional items such as pins and catches.

SILVER AND GOLD

The two principal metals commonly used are silver and gold in alloy forms. They have both colour and sheen and are durable. Silver is the least costly precious metal. It is commonly alloyed with copper to produce sterling or standard silver in the ratio of 925 parts silver and 75 parts copper by weight. This produces a stronger metal that is suitable for most jewellery. It can be made ductile by annealing and hard by work-hardening.

Similarly, gold used for jewellery is seldom pure and it is typically alloyed with copper and silver to produce different metal qualities and carats. The carat is a measure of the amount of pure gold by weight in the alloy, 24 carat being pure gold.

Carat	% Pure gold	% Other metals
24	100	–
22	91.7	8.3
18	75.0	25.0
14	58.4	41.6
9	37.5	62.5

Gold can be alloyed to produce a range of colours: red, yellow, white and green.

OTHER METALS

Copper is a useful low-cost material that can be worked in a similar way to silver. It is suitable for making metal jewellery and is particularly suitable for enamel work. It will tarnish and requires lacquering to retain a polished

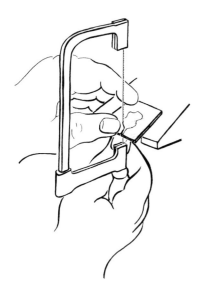

fig. 29
Sawing sheet material on a
bench pin using a
jeweller's saw.

fig. 30
Sawing out a large hole
from a drilled hole.

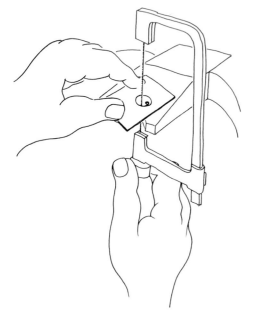

surface. The high melting point of copper makes it unsuitable for easy casting.

Aluminium alloys are also suitable but are more difficult to solder. They can, however, accept dyes and the surface can be protected by anodizing.

Zinc alloys cast well and are frequently used for costume jewellery, but give a metal that is too soft for some applications.

Refractory metals, such as **titanium**, **tantalum**, **niobium** and **zirconium** are not easy to work, but can be treated chemically and by heat to show a wide range of colours.

Stainless steel offers good colour and resists corrosion but, again, is not so easy to work.

Brass has an attractive yellow colour and combines well with copper but can fail when bent, although a ductile alloy is available from specialist suppliers.

Low-cost jewellery can be made from **tin plate** (tin-plated steel). It is easy to cut and fabricate and can easily be joined by soft soldering. Tin-plated copper combines well with tin plate.

Available forms   Gold, silver, copper, brass and aluminium alloys are available in sheet, wire, sections and granules. The various measurements and gauges by which metals are available are shown in the tables on pages 118–19. Jewellery can be built from sheet, wire or section and cast from granules or scrap.

FABRICATING TECHNIQUES

Sawing   The saw is one of the jeweller's most frequently used tools. It can be used to cut sheet material into intricate shapes both in outline and cut-out.

The first stage in the making of a sheet metal piece is the design, which should be worked out on paper and refined until acceptable.

There are a number of ways of transferring the drawn design on to the metal. One of the easiest is to transfer it on to a self-adhesive paper label by using carbon paper or tracing. Alternatively, the design may be drawn directly on to the label. Photographs and line drawings in magazines can often be cut out and stuck directly to the sheet metal. If the illustration is from a source which is is larger or smaller than required then photocopies (enlarged or reduced if necessary) can be used. Details for engraving or punching can be marked through from the drawing. For very fine work, the metal is painted with marking pen or engineers' blue and the design drawn on to this using a scriber.

The advantages of using self-adhesive labels are that the design can be positioned to the edges of the available metal, minimizing waste; also cutting through paper helps lubricate the saw blade.

The saw must be fitted with a blade suitable for the thickness of material being sawn (see page 120), its teeth pointing down towards the handle. First, clamp the blade at the handle end, then with the other end of the frame resting against the bench, clamp the other end. The frame is slightly sprung so that the blade is in tension, once both ends have been clamped.

Sawing is done on a bench pin. Hold the piece flat on the top of the pin in such a way that the line of cutting is over the gap. In the other hand hold the saw, the blade vertical (fig. 29).

The sawing action is a gentle, steady, up and down movement with the blade doing the work. Movement of the wrist guides the blade along the cutting line. When the saw blade nearly reaches the back of the cut-out in the bench pin, stop and bring the piece forward. Repeat the process until the job is completed. It is most important to keep the blade moving up and down *all the time* as this reduces the likelihood of it breaking.

To make cut-outs, a hole is drilled or punched within the area of the cut-out and near to the marked cutting line. One end of the saw blade can be released and the blade fed through the hole in the material with the design away from the saw handle. The blade is reclamped and sawing can proceed (fig. 30).

Acute inside shapes can be cut by sawing up into the corner, withdrawing the saw to the hole, or cutting a new hole, turning the piece 180°, and then moving the blade back into the corner so as to saw along the desired line.

Hand shears can be used to cut sheet metal but the cutting action distorts the sheet which then has to be flattened.

Making holes in sheet metal Holes can be drilled or punched. Drilling can be done with a variety of drills and drill bits. The traditional jewellers' drill has the great advantage of being used one-handed, leaving the other hand to hold the material (fig. 31). Powered pillar drills have the same advantage. Another type of drill is the Archimedes drill (fig. 32).

When using a small hand drill, wedge the material or clamp it to a piece of scrap wood heavy enough to resist the turning action of the drill. And to prevent the drill wandering across the surface, make a small centre-punched indentation by supporting the material on a firm surface and tapping the point of the punch with a light blow of the hammer where the hole is required.

Punching holes has the advantage of being quick and makes no waste. The simplest way of making punches is to file the end of a piece of silver steel, or even a nail, to the section of the hole required. The end of the punch must be flat and the edges sharp. With the material set firmly on a yielding surface, such as a piece of hardboard, which itself is resting on a firm surface, the punch is

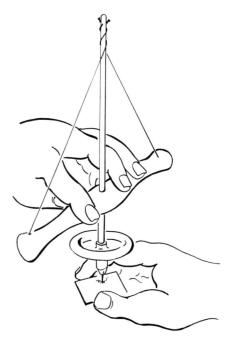

fig. 31
Drilling a hole using a traditional jeweller's drill.

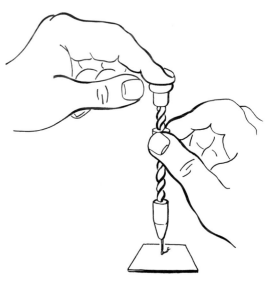

fig. 32
Drilling with an Archimedes drill.

**fig. 33
Punching a hole using a
flat-ended, sharp-edged
punch.**

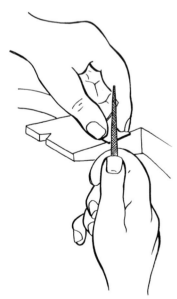

**fig. 34
Filing the edge of a piece of
sheet metal.**

struck very firmly with a single blow which should drive out a slug of metal in the shape of the end of the punch (fig. 33). The process is only suitable for thin sheet.

Filing   Swiss files can be used to smooth the edges of sheet metal. The piece can be laid flat on the bench pin just overlapping the edge. Filing is done with a gentle up and down motion holding the file square to the face of the material and at a slight angle to vertical (fig. 34).

A good general-purpose file is a half-round Swiss file, which can be used for flat faces, outward and inward curves and sharp corners. Round, flat and triangular sections are among the many varieties available.

Wire cutting   Wire can be cut to length with shears or cutters. The type of cutting head will determine the shape of the cut face. Sawn wire will need to be dressed with a file to remove burrs and square the end.

Forming wire   Copper, silver and gold wire forms easily when in a soft condition. Wire of up to about 1.5 mm diameter, can be easily formed with pliers. Smooth curves and rings are formed with round-nose pliers. For heavier sections half-round pliers with one flat blade and one half-round blade will prevent the indentation that can occur when using round-nose pliers.

For making corners use flat-nose pliers, but for a really sharp corner a V notch should be filed almost through and the joint soldered after bending.

To make large rings form the wire around a mandrel and for jump rings around a round steel rod.

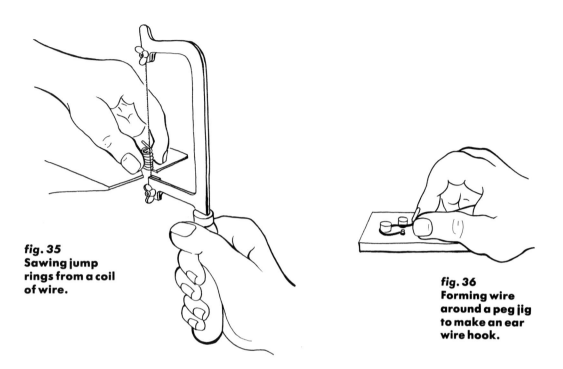

**fig. 35
Sawing jump
rings from a coil
of wire.**

**fig. 36
Forming wire
around a peg jig
to make an ear
wire hook.**

To make oval jump rings, form the wire around a mandrel then slightly squash the coiled piece in a vice to make an oval section before sawing through on one long edge (fig. 35).

For repeated shapes, simple jigs made from pegs, screws or nails driven into hard wood, will ensure consistency of shape. Fig. 36 shows ear wires being formed on a peg jig.

Interest can be added to formed wire by forging it flat after bending it to shape. Apart from altering the section, this also hardens the material. Simple pin designs make very effective pieces of jewellery and are easy to make by forming wire and hammering the end flat to form the catch (fig. 37).

Work-hardening wire   After forming and soldering operations, it is sometimes desirable to re-harden wire. With square- or rectangular-section wire, alternately hammering on adjacent sides will work-harden the material while retaining the section. For round wire it is possible to hammer the wire, rotating it at the same time, although this can cause too much deformation. An alternative method is to twist the wire, which introduces a stretching of the material and work-hardens it without losing the round section.

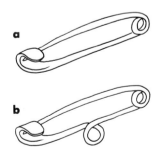

**fig. 37
a) Simple pin design made
from round wire with
forged end.
b) simple pin incorporating
a suspension loop.**

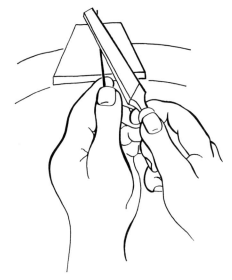

**fig. 38
Filing wire to a
taper.**

Drawing It is possible to shape wire and also to reduce it in section (i.e. make it thinner) by pulling it through holes in a draw plate.

The principle advantage of this process is that you do not have to keep all gauges of wire in stock and it allows you to use up melted scrap by first rolling it to a square section and then drawing it.

To draw down a piece of wire the end must first be tapered either by filing (fig. 38) or, more easily, by hammering it flat and cutting a point using shears.

The draw plate is mounted in a vice or draw bench and the tapered end of wire inserted through the hole next down in size to the wire's present gauge.

The wire is then pulled through the tapered hole with the use of draw tongs (fig. 39). This operation is repeated until the required size is reached. Because the metal work-hardens during the process it will require annealing.

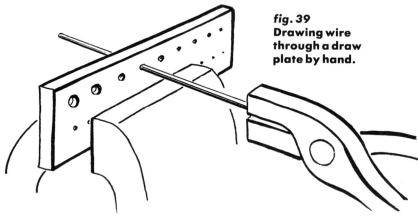

**fig. 39
Drawing wire
through a draw
plate by hand.**

**fig. 40
Forming strip
around bars
held in a vice**

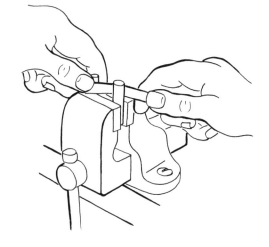

Forming sheet metal Narrow sections of sheet metal can be formed in similar ways to wire. Fig. 40 shows strip metal being formed around bars held in a vice.

To form a sharp corner in sheet a V groove is made almost through the metal and the joint soldered after bending (fig. 41). U-section sheet can be produced by forming in a swage block using round steel bars (fig. 42). Circular domes can be formed from discs using a doming block and punch (fig. 43). Irregular three-dimensional shapes are formed with repoussé punches. For this process the annealed metal sheet is warmed and set on to the surface of a pitch bowl. When cool, the design is punched forward with hammer and punches. As the work progresses, the metal will work-harden and require annealing. Sharp inside corners are achieved by removing the piece from the pitch, back filling the hollow back of the piece with pitch and resetting it the right way up on the pitch block. Punches can then be used to crisp up the detail.

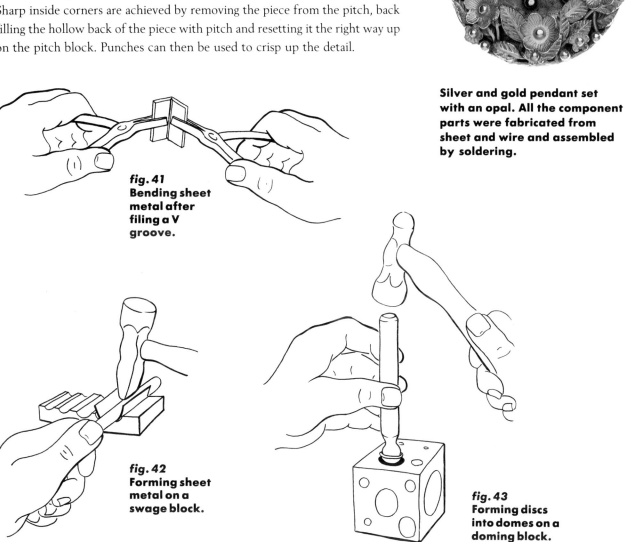

Silver and gold pendant set with an opal. All the component parts were fabricated from sheet and wire and assembled by soldering.

**fig. 41
Bending sheet metal after filing a V groove.**

**fig. 42
Forming sheet metal on a swage block.**

**fig. 43
Forming discs into domes on a doming block.**

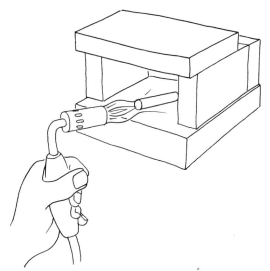

fig. 44
Simple hearth built up from fire bricks and used to contain the heat during high temperature operations such as annealing. Note that a gap is left at the top, to the back of the hearth to allow hot gases to escape.

Annealing metal   To enable metal to be easily worked it is made soft by annealing. The table below shows the heating and cooling temperatures appropriate to different metals.

Metal	Heating	Cooling
Silver	raise to 600°C	quench in pickle or water
Gold	raise to 650°C	air-cool slowly to 200°C, quench, pickle when cold
Copper	raise to 800°C	quench in water or pickle
Steel	raise to 800°C	air-cool slowly

Fig. 44 shows a simple hearth in which annealing can be done using a gas torch.

Punching shapes   Circular shapes can be made with punches. This is done with the sheet metal resting on a resilient pad to protect the cutting edge of the punch (fig. 45).

About 6 mm of newspaper or magazines is suitable but the paper must rest on a very solid anvil. Small shapes in thin sheet metal can be punched out using flat-ended, sharp-edged punches.

Using punches for decoration   Punches can be bought or made quite simply from lengths of silver steel, or even from cut-down nails, by filing and polishing the end.

By resting the metal sheet on a firm base, repeated shaped indentations can be made. Crisp flat-bottomed indentation will result if the metal being worked is set on a heavy, smooth metal anvil. If it is set in pitch or on a fibre board sheet, the indentations will be more rounded at the edges and deeper. These rounded corners can be sharpened up by turning the piece over and tapping the identations from behind, which is the basis of repoussé and chasing work.

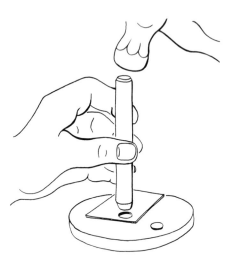

fig. 45
Hole-cutting and disc-making using hollow-ended, sharp-edged punch on a yielding surface.

Surface finish   The basic finish for metals is normally a smooth polished surface. If the piece has been fabricated then the cut and shaped surfaces will show the marks of the cutting and forming tools, which in most cases have to be smoothed out. If the piece has been soldered, then there is often surface discoloration, or fire stain in the case of silver, to remove.

Finishing is a progressive process of refining the quality of the surface to obtain a good 'finish'. The following list shows a range of finishing methods and materials for metal jewellery.

Method/material	Process
Filing	rub with Swiss files of various cross-sections.
Emery cloth and wet-and-dry paper	rubbing with fine grades of either of these will give a uniform finish. Flat surfaces are worked by placing the sheet on a hard flat surface and working the piece over in a figure of eight motion. For working inside curves or cut-outs, the abrasive sheet can be glued around a length of wooden dowel.
Silicon carbide powder	wet and brush on with an old toothbrush to coarse finish inside intricate shapes.
Rouge powder	rub on (dry) with a polishing cloth.
Burnishing	using a soap solution and a burnishing tool to smooth edges and surfaces.

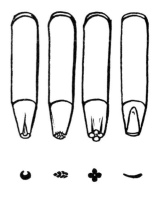

fig. 46
Selection of hand-made indenting punches.

JOINING METAL COMPONENTS

Simple pieces of jewellery can be made from one piece of metal. More frequently different shapes and sections are made and then assembled by one of the following methods.

fig. 47
Punches used in combination can produce attractive patterns.

Method	Application
Bending and twisting	winding wire and thin strip formed back on itself to make loops or folds (e.g. jump rings)
Riveting	deforming the end of a wire or rivet to form a head
Swaging	forming over the edge of thin sheet to trap an enclosed component (e.g. stone setting)
Force fitting	making an interference fit between two components and driving one into the other
Screw threads	forming or cutting screw threads to make studs, screws and nuts
Hard and soft soldering	creating a bond between two touching components with solder
Bonding with adhesive	sticking components together with adhesive, such as an epoxy resin

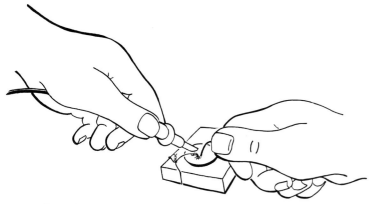

fig. 48
Soft soldering a brooch finding in place. The finding is positioned with iron binding wire.

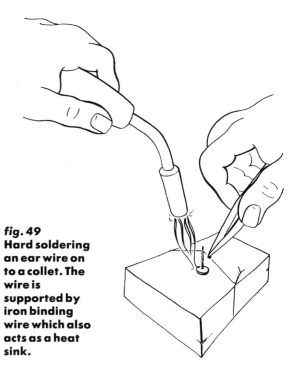

fig. 49
Hard soldering an ear wire on to a collet. The wire is supported by iron binding wire which also acts as a heat sink.

Soldering There are two main types of soldering: hard and soft.

In **soft soldering**, which is suitable for working copper, brass and tinned steel, a tin-based alloy with a melting point of about 180°C is used. Cored solder (i.e. containing its own flux core) used for electronic work is suitable.

Make sure there is a good joint or contact face between the pieces to be joined and that the touching faces are clean. If necessary clean them with emery paper or an abrasive block.

The components, set on a heat-proof non-metal (e.g. charcoal or ceramic) surface, are tinned by heating them with an electrical soldering iron and, when hot, touching them with solder at the point of the join. A thin layer of solder will flow over the surface. The components should be cleaned of any excess solder when cool. Now position the components, using iron binding wire or other improvised supports. Heating them with a soldering iron will melt the tinned faces and produce a joint (fig. 48).

For tinning large areas, the tip of the iron is run over the surface of the component. For small joints the cleaned components can be positioned, heated and will bond by the application of a touch of solder.

Silver brooches, necklace and earrings, all fabricated from sheet and wire and assembled by hard soldering.

Hard soldering is appropriate for silver and gold pieces.

Hard solder is available in easy, medium, hard and enamelling grades. Easy has the lowest melting point and enamelling the highest. For most work, medium solder is suitable. If the piece is to be hallmarked gold or silver in accordance with the Hallmarking Act 1973, then appropriate hallmarking quality solder must be used.

The process is similar to soft soldering except that the flux (preferably in liquid form which flows more easily and is easier to remove after soldering) has to be applied separately and the temperatures are much higher, typically 800°C. To obtain these high temperatures the metal must be heated with a gas torch.

The cleaned components are positioned and a flux applied to the joint. The assembly is heated and when the soldering temperature is reached (dull red heat) a small paillon of solder is applied to the joint (fig. 49). If the joint is clean, well fluxed and the temperature correct, the solder will instantly flow along the joint in a shiny thread.

Silver pieces can, with care, be quenched straight away in pickle to remove the residue of flux but gold pieces must be allowed to cool before quenching.

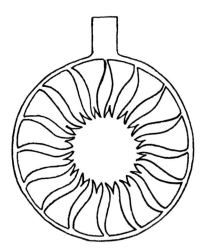

fig. 50
Pierced metal sun
pendant.

fig. 51
The shape of the
pendant is
domed and the
tab formed
over.

PROJECT 1

PIERCED METAL SUN PENDANT

Tools and Equipment

Bench pin

Piercing saw and blades (size 1/0)

Self-adhesive labels or plain paper
  and glue

Pencil, fine ballpoint pen and pair
  of compasses

Drill and 1 mm diameter drill bit

Centre punch

Half-round Swiss file

Hammer with ball and flat face

Piece of soft wood for use as a
  doming block

Round-nose pliers

Fine grade wet-and-dry paper

Polish and polishing equipment

Lacquer (for base metals)

Materials

Silver, copper, brass or aluminium sheet 50 mm square and between 0.5 mm
and 1 mm thick (20–24swg)

Method

With the aid of the compasses, draw the design in pencil and when you have
achieved a satisfactory layout line it in with a fine ballpoint pen. (N.B. the
projecting tab [fig. 50] will later be bent over to form a hanging point.) Stick
the drawing down on to the metal. If you have drawn on a self-adhesive label
this process will be simple.

  Centre-punch and then drill a hole in each area of the design to be cut out.
Thread the saw blade through a hole, clamp it and cut the shape out. Repeat
for all the cut-outs. Now cut round the outer edge of the design and remove
the paper.

  Correct any mis-sawn shape by filing and lightly rounding all edges.

  Smooth the whole piece with wet-and-dry paper and give it a first polish.
(The cut-outs are polished by moving the piece along a taut, polish-dressed
hank of thread.)

  Now, using the ball of the hammer, gently dome the piece from the back.
Using round-nose pliers form the tab over to make a hanging point (fig. 51).

  The piece can now be finish polished. Silver needs no treatment, but other
base metals should be lacquered. Finally, hang the piece on a twisted cord,
thong or chain.

PROJECT 2

PIERCED AND PAINTED ALUMINIUM EARRINGS

Tools and Equipment

Bench pin

Piercing saw and blades (size 2/0)

Self-adhesive labels or plain paper
    and glue

Pencil, ballpoint pen and drawing
    instruments

Drill and 1 mm diameter drill bit

Centre punch

Half-round Swiss file

Hammer

Fine wet-and-dry paper

Length of fine wire

Materials

Aluminium sheet, 1–1.5 mm (16–18 swg) 25×50 mm

Solder   Can of spray paint   Ear wires

Method

The basic method of drawing and cutting out the design is the same as in
Project 1 but since the shapes are geometric more precision is required in
cutting out. Smooth all edges, clean the surfaces and give them a satin finish as
a key for the paint.

Next suspend the pieces from a length of thin wire and spray them with car
touch-up paint. This is best done outside on a dry still day.

Once the paint is dry, ear wires can be fitted. Twist the hook open, thread it
through and twist closed.

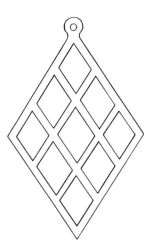

**fig. 52
Pierced and
painted
aluminium
earring design.**

a

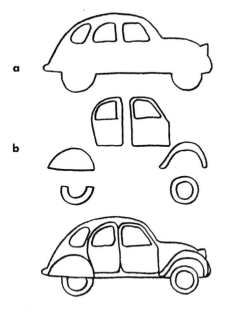

b

**fig. 53
Car brooch design.**

PROJECT 3
CAR BROOCH

Tools and Equipment

Bench pin

Piercing saw and blades (size 2/0)

Plain paper and glue

Pencil, ballpoint pen

Drill and 1 mm drill bit

Centre punch

Hammer

Half-round Swiss file

Soldering equipment

Fine wet-and-dry paper

Can of spray paint

(for base metals)

Polishing equipment

Materials

Silver, aluminium, brass or copper sheet, 1–1.5 mm (16–18 swg).
Standard brooch pin finding.

Method

This piece is built up from sheet in two layers, each layer joined by soldering or an adhesive.

Draw the design (see fig. 53) and make three copies of it (you will need three copies to cut out all the shapes). This is most easily done by photocopying or alternatively by tracing using carbon paper. Stick the entire design (a) and elements from the design (b) on to the sheet metal. Cut out and pierce (a) as in Projects 1 and 2. Then cut out (b), i.e. the mudguard, door and wheel shapes.

Join the component pieces together, hard soldering silver, soft soldering copper and brass and sticking aluminium with epoxy resin. Finish polish. Fit a commercial brooch pin to the back by soldering or adhesive, as appropriate, and either polish or (in the case of base metals) spray paint.

PROJECT 4

EARRINGS IN CONTRASTING METALS

Tools and Equipment

Bench pin

Piercing saw and blades (size 2/0)

Pencil, ballpoint pen and paper

Scribe

File

Pliers, flat- and round-nose

Fine wet-and-dry paper

Soldering equipment

Water of Ayr stone and water

Polish and polishing equipment

Materials

Sheet metal, 0.5 mm (25 swg): gold (red, yellow and white) or brass, copper and German silver. Each piece a rectangle 35×10 mm.

Solder   2 small jump rings   Ear wires

Method

Each earring is built up from three overlapped layers of metal in contrasting colours. In precious metal a good contrast is achieved with red, yellow and white gold. Brass, copper and German silver offer a cheaper alternative.

Draw the design of each piece in full (fig. 54) and transfer it on to the metal. Rather than actually gluing the paper on to the metal, you can scribe lines directly on to the metal surface, which allows for more precision in the marking out. After cutting out, make the edges straight and true by rubbing on a sheet of fine wet-and-dry paper resting on a hard, flat surface. Now solder component parts. There will be a tendency for the capillary forces in the solder to pull the pieces across each other. This can be prevented by gripping the pieces together with soldering tweezers as each joint is made or by positioning the components with pins driven into the soldering board.

Next solder small jump rings to the top end of each earring and remove solder from the visible surfaces, using a well-wetted water of Ayr stone. Polish the piece and fit ear wires.

**fig. 54
Earrings in contrasting metals. Marking out the sheet.**

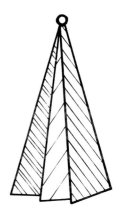

**fig. 55
Arrangement of the earring pieces for soldering.**

PROJECT 5

OXIDIZED SILVER FISH BROOCH

Tools and Equipment

Bench pin

Bench vice

Anvil

Piercing saw and blades (size 2/0)

Half-round Swiss file

Drill and 2 mm diameter twist drill

2 short lengths of silver steel or mild
   steel, 4–6 mm diameter

Centre punch

Torch, charcoal block and
   equipment for silver soldering

Water of Ayr stone and water

Flat-nose pliers

Polishing equipment

Paper, pencil, ballpoint pen
   and glue

Pickle tweezers

Kitchen paper

Old toothbrush or small paintbrush

Materials

Silver sheet 0.5 mm thick (25 swg) 40×40 mm

Silver solder   Potassium sulphide   Acid pickle and water container

**fig. 56
Oxidized silver
fish brooch.**

Method

This fish brooch (fig. 56) is built up from a number of components, assembled
by soldering.

First, draw the fish, making it 2 mm larger all round than the required
finished size. Glue the design on to the sheet of silver and cut out. This forms
the back face on to which the scales, head and fins will be soldered.

Peel the paper design off and reuse it on some of the remaining sheet for
cutting out the fish head and eye.

It is now necessary to make a hollow-ended punch for shaping the eye.
Centre-punch the end of a piece of silver steel or, if this is not available, mild

steel and, holding it in a bench vice, drill the end some 2 mm to 3 mm deep with a 2 mm drill. Smooth the edges lightly.

Placing the head-shaped piece of silver on a solid smooth metal anvil punch the eye shape firmly into the metal. Any distortion of the shape can be corrected by filing.

Now hard solder the head piece on to the main body and saw out the large lower fin from the cut away silver sheet.

The remaining sheet provides material for the scales when it has been cut into small pieces about 2–3 mm square. (The shape is not critical.)

These small pieces are placed on a charcoal block and heated with a gas torch until they melt into small spheres. While they are still hot, quench them in pickle, wash them in water and dry them. Then flatten them by hammering them on an anvil.

Take up each flattened bead in smooth-jawed pliers and file two edges at right angles. A few of the beads, for positioning next to the head, are only given one straight edge.

Now solder the scales (pickled, washed and dried) on to the back face. Flux the body of the fish and arrange the scales in place.

Heat (gently at first to minimize the chance of the scales moving) until the scales become soldered in position. Pickle, wash and dry.

Make a second tool by flattening a piece of steel with a hammer and filing the end into a chisel shape. This simple punch is used to stamp the spines on the fins. Apply solder to the back of the large lower fin, position and solder it on to the scales.

Now carefully saw the final outline to shape, shaping all the fins. The shape of the mouth is made by filing. Smooth the file marks away with water of Ayr stone and now smooth and polish the whole piece. The faces of the gaps between the fins can be polished with wet silicon carbide powder and a toothbrush.

Solder a brooch hinge finding on the back at the head end and a thick open jump ring at the other, then rivet on a standard pin with a short length of silver wire.

To harden the jump ring, support it on the edge of the anvil and lightly hammer it. Then trim the opening and polish the whole piece.

The piece is now oxidized and finish polished as in Chapter 5.

5 Metals: Colouring, Electroforming and Etching

METAL COLOURING

Brass, copper and silver can be coloured by treating the surface with chemicals and heat. The range of colours that can be achieved is, however, fairly limited.

The refractory metals, niobium, tantalum, titanium and zinanium, can be treated electrolytically and with heat to produce a very full spectrum of bright colours.

Steel, iron, copper and brass can be electroplated with silver and gold. Copper and brass can also be tinned.

All these methods require careful use of chemicals, heat, or both. The electrolytic methods require specialized equipment.

CHEMICAL COLOURING

Brass   Brass can be coloured in the range of red, purple, brown, black, blue-green, green and yellow. The processes are as follows.

Colour	Solution	Treatment
Purple	Copper nitrate 80 g Ammonia 4 cc Water 1 litre	Immerse for 30 minutes in boiling solution. Wash in hot water and protect with a wax finish.
Purple Brown	Copper sulphate 25 g Ammonia 3 cc Water 1 litre	Immerse for 30 minutes in boiling solution. Wash in hot water. Wax finish.
Reddish Brown	Copper acetate 50 g Copper nitrate 50 g Water 1 litre	Immerse for 30 minutes in boiling solution. Wash in hot water. Wax finish.

Black	Copper carbonate 170 g
	Ammonia 350 cc
	Water 1 litre
		Immerse for up to 60
		   minutes. Wash in
		   warm water only.
		   Wax with care.

Blue-green	Copper nitrate
	Water 1 litre
		Heat and immerse in
		   solution. Repeat.
		   Wax on cooling.

Yellow/Orange	Copper sulphate 25 g
	Ammonia 4 cc
	Water 1 litre
		Immerse for a few
		   minutes. Observe.
		   Wax when dry.

Copper   Copper can be coloured in the red, brown, black and blue-green range by the following methods.

Colour	Solution	Treatment

Red	Water	Heat the piece and plunge
		   quickly into boiling water.
		   Finish by waxing.

Brown	Ferric chloride 10 gm
	Water 1 litre
		Heat the piece and apply
		   solution with scratch
		   brush. Wash and wax.

Black	Barium sulphide 10 gm
	Water 1 litre
		Leave for 2 hours in cold
		   solution. Wash, dry and
		   wax.

Blue-
  green
	Copper nitrate 200 gm
	Water 1 litre
		Heat the piece and apply the
		   solution with a brush,
		   wash, dry and wax.

Textured silver earrings with an oxidized background which contrasts with the raised and polished design.

Silver   Silver can be given a blue/black or grey patina.

Colour	Solution	Treatment
Blue/black	Potassium sulphide 10 gm Water 1 litre	Warm the piece and touch with the solution. Watch the colour change and stop by immersing in clean water.
Grey	Potassium sulphide 3 gm Ammonium carbonate 6 gm	Immerse in cold solution for a few minutes.

Other methods   The refractory metal **titanium** can be coloured (once the surface has been etched) by the simple process of heating with a torch, which produces oxides on the surface. However, over-heating can create dull colours and some practice is required to create clear, bright colours. The process has the advantage of requiring a minimum of equipment.

Titanium, **niobium** and **tantalum** can be coloured by an electrolytic process, best carried out in an electroplating bath. An electrolyte of 10 percent ammonium sulphate is used. The piece to be coloured is cleaned with acetone and attached as the anode (+); platinized titanium is used as the cathode (−). Varying the voltage will change the colour. Make test pieces at different voltages to discover how to produce specific colours. Colours can be stopped out using varnish or nail polish.

Base metals can be electroplated with copper, silver and gold. Better adhesion is achieved with an initial coating of copper on most metals. If you do not have electroplating facilities or access to a commercial plater it is possible to create a thin plated surface using proprietary plating polishes and dips.

Copper and **brass** can be hot tinned by applying solder to the heated piece, then wiping the surface with a heavy cloth to spread the solder. If the surface is indented or heavily textured, good contrast can be achieved by polishing the high points of solder away.

ELECTROFORMING

Complicated three-dimensional shapes not easy to cast or fabricate can be created by electroforming. Either made-up models or natural forms, such as leaves, nuts and berries, can be metal-coated. The metal is deposited electrolytically in a plating bath until a sufficient thickness is built up.

First cut the shape out of an easily workable material: three possibilities are expanded polystyrene, papier-mâché and balsa wood. As the piece will have to be immersed in an electrolyte, you will need to weight the centre of the model to stop it floating. When you have finished shaping and modelling, fit a wire from which to suspend the piece. With earrings, for example, this can become part of the finished piece. Seal the model with a suitable lacquer or varnish and, when it is dry, paint the piece with a conductive paint, which is generally rich in silver powder. Alternatively, carbon or graphite dust can be used, set in the wet varnish.

The easiest way to have the model heavily plated is to use the services of a commercial plating company or use a plating bath, but if necessary you can use an improvised arrangement as follows.

Take a rigid plastic container which will easily hold the model. Fit two copper or brass rods across the top and wire the model via its wire hanger to one bar – the cathode. To the other bar wire a piece of copper sheet, e.g. copper plumbing pipe. Now fill the container with a saturated solution of copper sulphate and a little vinegar. To the two bars attach a 1.5 volt dry battery, positive to the anode, negative to the cathode (see fig. 57). Now wait. Over a period of a few days a substantial coating of copper will be built up from the copper anode onto the model. When the coating is sufficiently thick, the battery and conductors can be removed and the coated piece washed in water. Burnishing will improve the surface finish.

The model may be simply suspended for earrings or a pendant or if the metal coating is thick enough, fabricated into a more complex piece.

The piece can now be varnished or silver or gold plated.

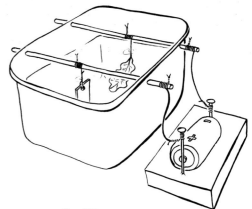

**fig. 57
Improvised electroforming bath.**

ETCHING

Selected acids will attack and eat away metal. This action can be used to create relief designs. However, acids are dangerous. They can burn and the fumes are harmful if inhaled. Great care and suitable protection particularly for the hands, face and eyes is essential. Any work with acids should be carried out in a well-ventilated area.

Copper and silver sheet are suitable metals on which to practise etching. The recessed design created can simply be left textured and the untouched surface polished. Alternatively, the recessed part can be chemically coloured, enamelled or filled with coloured resin.

Etching involves not only a mordant (i.e. the acid) to eat away some of the metal but also a 'resist' to protect the parts that are not to be etched.

There are a number of resists, two of which are particularly recommended: a resist pen, as used by electronic engineers, and, for coating larger areas and

**fig. 59
Etching in
prepared
acid.**

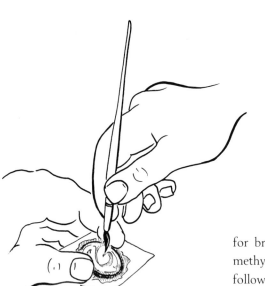

**fig. 58
Painting a resist pattern.**

for brushwork designs, common red sealing wax, crushed and soaked in methylated spirit. All surfaces that are not to be etched need protection. The following technique is speedy and effective.

Make a solution of sealing wax the consistency of thin cream and with it coat a piece of paper greater than the size of the metal to be etched. On this, and while it is still wet, lay the piece of metal face up, ensuring the metal is in full contact with the resist. Now brush the sealing wax resist up the edges of the metal and around the edge of the top face to form a frame. The backing paper will provide a convenient means of lifting the piece without getting sticky fingers.

Draw or paint the prepared design onto the remaining metal surface using a resist (fig. 58) and allow the whole to dry.

As a mordant for copper, use solution of one part sulphuric acid to two parts water; for silver, two parts nitric acid to one part water. Weaker solutions will take longer to etch.

Always add acid to water – not water to acid. Adding water to acid can cause a violent action, splashing acid.

Pyrex dishes are suitable for holding the prepared acid (fig. 59) but should not then be used for any other purpose. You will also need a dish of clean water for washing, and a supply of kitchen paper for drying.

Use tongs made of copper, plastic or bamboo – not other metals – for lifting the piece in and out of the acid.

Lift the piece into the acid. When the etching process starts, small bubbles will form on the metal surface and rise up. To encourage this action and help ensure an even etch, tickle the metal surface with the tip of a feather (fig. 60).

The depth of etching can be judged by feeling it with a wooden toothpick, taking care not to damage the resist. When an acceptable depth of etching has been achieved, lift the piece out carefully, wash and dry it. Clean off the resist with methylated spirit and the piece is ready for finishing.

**fig. 60
Feather tip for
removing
etching
bubbles.**

PROJECT 1

COPPERED LEAF EARRINGS

Tools and Equipment

Small plastic container
1.5 volt battery
Battery connectors and insulated
 wire
Copper sulphate
Vinegar

Varnish
Graphite, copper powder or
 conductive paint
Piece of clean copper
 (tube or heavy wire)

Materials

Small leaves

Copper wire

Method

Dry the leaf and wind the copper wire around the stalk, forming a loop by which to suspend it in the solution.

Now lightly varnish the leaf and when still tacky cover in graphite or copper powder. Alternatively paint with conductive paint. If you have difficulty in obtaining these materials, powdered pencil lead (produced by rubbing the lead on a file) will produce a suitable alternative.

Put about 2 cm of water into the container and add a few drops of vinegar and copper sulphate crystals until no more will dissolve.

Using the insulated electrical wire, connect the wire loop on the leaf to the negative (−) side of the battery and the positive (+) side to the piece of copper. Now be patient. During the plating process, turn the leaf over and around in the bath to ensure an even coating. In about two days (the process is quicker if the whole apparatus is kept warm) a layer of copper will have built up on the leaf, which can now be disconnected, dried, washed and lightly polished with a silver cloth.

Finally attach suitable ear wires.

These earrings are made from natural seeds and leaves which have been wired, coated and electroplated. The plated components are linked by chain and fitted with ear wires.

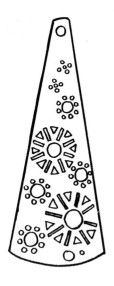

**fig. 61
Oxidized
earring design.**

PROJECT 2
OXIDIZED EARRINGS AND MATCHING PENDANT

Tools and Equipment

Bench pin   Chisel punch
Saw and blades (size 2/0)   Round flat-ended punch
Hammer   Polishing materials (a silver cloth)
Anvil   Drill and 1 mm diameter drill bit

Materials

Silver sheet 1.5 mm thick (16 swg)   Watercolour brush and water pot
Potassium sulphide   Steel rod for punches
                                       Ear wires

Method

This project is as much an exercise in punching indented decorations as in metal colouring.

Cut out the basic shapes, smooth, and polish them.

Make a punch for each punched shape (see pages 32–3).

The position of the indentations can be marked using a fine permanent felt-tip pen. If you make a mistake, rub it out with an eraser and start again!

Position the metal shape on the anvil. (If the surface of the anvil is less than perfect, protect the back of the piece with two or three layers of masking tape.) Position the end of the punch with care, holding it firmly on to the metal surface. Then with a heavy hammer strike one firm blow. The punch needs to go about half way into the metal. Make sure it has not moved out of position if you need to strike again. Continue until the design is complete.

The punch will have raised the edges of the indentation. These ridges are removed by rubbing the surface over a sheet of fine wet-and-dry paper laid on a hard, smooth surface. This will give a clean sharp edge to the design. Re-shape any edge distortion.

Drill the top holes after first centre punching. Now polish the piece, wash it clean and colour it, as described on page 44.

When the colouring is complete, polish the top face to create contrast.

Copper and brass may be substituted for silver, using the appropriate chemicals. The basic metal work can also be coloured by enamelling (see Chapter 10).

Finally, fit suitable ear wires.

PROJECT 3
ETCHED AND COLOURED COPPER NECKPIECE

Tools and Equipment

Tin snips

File

Polishing equipment

Round-nose pliers

Pyrex dish

Nitric acid (20% solution in water)

Hammer

Lead block

Resist and solvent

Paper, pencil and paint brush

Copper nitrate

Materials

Copper sheet about 1.5 mm thick
  (16 swg)

Silk or rayon for the cord

8 beads

2 crimps

Fastenings –
  bolt ring and jump ring

Method

Lay out the design on paper to ensure that the individual plaques will hang well together.

Mark out each plaque on the sheet metal (fig. 63) either directly or using labels or paper. (Don't forget the top tabs.)

Coat the back with resist, drawing it up to protect the edges and make a frame (see pages 45–6). Now paint in the desired raised design and when this is dry suspend the pieces in the etching solution. When etching has been achieved polish the top faces and chemically colour the recesses. Form over the top tabs with round-nose pliers. This design of necklace can be hung on a twisted thread cord, commercially-made cord, leather thong or chain.

fig. 62
Etched and coloured copper necklace.

fig. 63
Economic layout of the necklace shapes for cutting, showing the tabs.

6 Stones

The gem stones used in jewellery can be roughly divided into precious, semi-precious, synthetic and imitation. They are also grouped for hardness on the Mohs scale. This is useful in that it gives an indication of how easy or difficult a stone is to cut and how well it will wear. Garnet, for example, is a relatively hard stone (7–7½ on the Mohs scale) and malachite is quite soft (3½–4 on Mohs scale).

Numerous stones are suitable for jewellery. A simplified list of the precious category gives diamonds, the corundum group of sapphire and ruby and the beryl group of emerald and aquamarine.

Among the more popular semi-precious stones are agate, amethyst, aventurine, bloodstone, blue lace agate, carnelian, garnet, goldstone, haematite, jade, malachite, onyx, snowflake obsidian, sodalite and tiger eye. These are all quite easy to shape and polish on a lapidary machine or can be purchased ready-polished from suppliers.

In addition to these, and probably to be classed in the semi-precious group, are pearls, coral, amber, mother-of-pearl shell and the more colourful awabe and paua shells. Shell can be worked with normal metal-working tools and is easy to polish.

Selection of precious stones.

Synthetic stones are manmade but with the same or similar characteristics of chemical composition, hardness and refractive index as the natural stones. They have the advantage of both lower price and freedom from the flaws or inclusions that are often found in natural stones.

Imitation stones are low-cost imitations of natural stones often made from coloured glass, sometimes called paste.

Gem stones are generally cut in one of two ways, faceted or cabochon.

As a general rule (though there are exceptions) transparent stones are faceted, i.e. cut and polished with multiple facets to give them sparkle and colour. Opaque or translucent stones are cabochon cut, i.e. cut with a flat back and a domed top. Stones can also simply be tumble-polished, resulting in what is called a baroque shape.

It is possible to buy rough rock, crystals and boules and cut, grind and polish them to shape. This approach has the advantage of being able to make a stone of a non-standard size or shape and to maximize a stone's particular characteristic. It does, however, take time and requires specialized machinery for anything more than a very simple shape.

Commercially cut stones, both faceted and cabochon cut, in natural and synthetic material are available in a range of standard sizes. These have the advantage of fitting standard collets and settings.

Imitation stones in coloured glass, plain and mirror-backed, are available at very low cost in most colours and many shapes.

PEBBLE POLISHING

The simplest, but most time-consuming method (and that used in ancient times) is hand-grinding and polishing. The advantage is that the equipment costs are almost nil, but a strong right arm is necessary. The small selected pebble is held between finger and thumb and, using a figure of eight movement, rubbed over a glass plate coated with a coarse silicon carbide paste. Repeated rubbing will grind away a flat face, and by using progressively finer silicon carbide paste, a smoother finish can be achieved. When the shape is right, polishing is continued using wetted aluminium or tin oxide on the smooth side of a piece of hardboard. It is possible to produce a roughly faceted stone by this method – but it takes time.

If the basic shape of the pebble is to be retained, then barrelling is used. The equipment consists of a rotating barrel into which the pebbles are put, together with a cutting agent (e.g. silicon carbide) and water. The abrasive action of the cutting agent gradually wears away and smooths the pebbles. Progressively finer cutting and polishing agents will bring the pebbles up to a high gloss. This process also takes time.

SETTING AND MOUNTING STONES

There are two basic ways to mount stones: bezel set and claw set, and there are many variations on these two basic approaches. There are also other and more specialized methods.

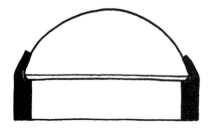

fig. 64
Section of a cabochon stone set in a bezel.

Bezel setting   A bezel setting is normally but not exclusively used for setting cabochon stones. It gives a continuous metal frame encircling the stone, providing either a rim (fig. 64) or a complete base (fig. 65) on which the stone sits.

The raised wall is formed by pushing the frame over the stone to retain it.

A wide range of commercial collets is available to suit calibrated standard-size stones, either faceted or cabochon. These are cast or pressed from sheet metal and can have a smooth or millgrain edge. They can be soldered to a piece of jewellery prior to setting the stone, but if you do this always check first that the stone sits snugly in place. If more than one collet is used, space them far enough apart to allow for the edges to be formed over all round.

fig. 65
Section of a cabochon stone set in a bezel of sheet metal, providing a complete base.

Claw setting   Normally used for faceted stones, a claw setting allows light to reach all the facets, thus maximizing a stone's sparkle. There are small ledges on the inside of the claws on which to set the stone; the tops of the claws are formed over to retain it.

PROJECT 1

CUTTING A CABOCHON

Tools and Equipment

Lapidary machine with saw, fine and coarse grinding wheels, expanding sanding disc and polishing disc

Flat-nose pliers

Polishes

Dop wax and dop sticks

Template and marking stick

Heater for dopping

Materials

Rough rock or slabs

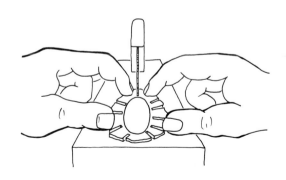

fig. 66
Sawing radial slots on the marked slab with a diamond saw.

Method

Use the diamond saw to cut the rough rock into a slab some 2 mm to 3 mm thicker than the height of the finished stone. On one face, the shape of the stone is marked out, which is conveniently done using a template and aluminium marking stick.

If only a small amount of material has to be removed, this can be done by grinding. If a large amount of material has to be removed, radial cuts should be made nearly up to the marked line (fig. 66). The waste pieces can be broken off using pliers and the stone ground down to the line. This part of the process is carried out with the stone resting on the working table of the machine. Both sawing and grinding must be done with a supply of water both to keep the stone cool and to wash away residue.

The stone now has to be attached to a dop stick so that it can be held for grinding (fig. 67).

The dop stick is a wooden dowel the end of which is covered with a knob of dop wax. To apply this, melt some dop wax in a shallow tin over a low flame. Dip the dop stick into it and build up a knob of dop wax. While it is still soft, press it on to a smooth surface to create a platform to hold the stone.

Now heat the stone to the temperature at which it will soften wax. A suitable method is to set it on the base of an inverted can, ventilated by cutouts at its base, enclosing a candle.

The coated dop stick is now pressed on to the back face of the stone and the dop wax moulded to give support.

When cool, the stone can be ground down to shape, using first a coarse wheel then finishing on a fine wheel. Grinding marks can be sanded away on an expanding sanding wheel. All these processes are carried out wet.

Finally the stone can be polished on a felt disc, using a progressively finer polish.

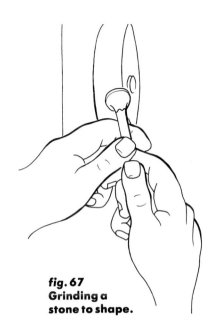

fig. 67
Grinding a stone to shape.

Selection of semi-precious
carbochon-cut stones and
polished slices of stone.

PROJECT 2
BEZEL-SET STONE BROOCH USING BEARER WIRE

Tools and Equipment

Bench pin	Half-round Swiss file
Shaped pliers, one jaw flat,	Anvil
one jaw half round	Riveting hammer
Jeweller's saw and blades (size 2/0)	Pusher and burnisher
Soldering torch	Polishing equipment
Soldering tweezers	

Materials

Length of bearer wire	Short length of wire for hook,
Cabochon stone	approx. 10×2×1 mm
Brooch pin and hinge	Solder

Method

Bearer wire is flat section, part thick part thin, creating, when formed round, a ledge on which the stone sits.

Using half-round pliers, form a length of bearer wire to fit closely around the stone. Saw off the overlapping ends, cutting through at a point to trim both ends (fig. 68). This ensures a good joint.

After checking that the stone is a good fit when the ends of the bearer wire touch, solder the ends together.

A commercial brooch pin hinge is now soldered at one end. It is convenient to file a small nick on the base of the bezel where the hinge is to fit to mark its position. A small amount of solder is melted on to the base of the hinge and a similar amount of solder applied to the mounted area of the bezel. With the bezel resting on a soldering block, the hinge is positioned, using soldering tweezers. Heating to soldering temperature will secure the hinge piece in place. Do not overheat the hinge.

Using a similar process, solder a rectangular strip in place which will be formed over into a hook. Now polish.

The brooch pin can now be fitted. First check that the hinge is clear of excess solder and will accept the pin. A short length of hinge wire is cut to project about half a diameter each side. Resting one face of the cross pin on an anvil, a riveting hammer is used on alternative ends to form over the rivet.

The stone can now be set. The raised bezel edge is pushed over at several place, using a gem-setting pusher (fig. 69). This is repeated, creating a gently rippled edge. Now using a burnisher, the edge is burnished over leaving a smooth bright edge (fig. 70). To support the piece during this operation, rest it across the part-open jaws of a vice or on a slotted piece of wood.

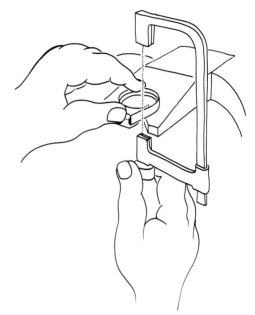

fig. 68
Cutting bearer wire to length after initial forming.

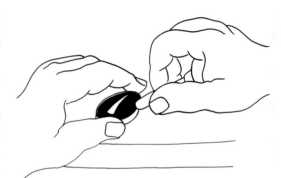

fig. 69
Pushing over the setting.

fig. 70
Burnishing over a stone setting.

**fig. 71
Claw-set,
single-faceted
stone ring.**

**fig. 72
Template for
claw collet
shown actual
size.**

**fig. 73
Formed collet
ready for hard
soldering.**

**fig. 74
Sawn and filed
collet.**

PROJECT 3

CLAW-SET, SINGLE-FACETED STONE RING

Tools and Equipment

Bench pin	Polishing equipment
Jeweller's saw and blades (size 2/0)	Pusher
Marking out equipment	Burnisher
Half-round Swiss file	Collet block and punch
Soldering equipment	Ring clamp

Materials

4 mm faceted round stone, e.g. amethyst, garnet, cubic zirconia
Sheet silver or gold
Shank material in silver or gold
Solder

Method

The starting point is the stone: for this project a 4 mm round stone has been selected. Once you have chosen the stone, you can make the claw collet.

A piece of silver or gold sheet is cut out to the shape of the template shown (fig. 72). Form the metal, using round-nose pliers and tapping the ends together on an anvil. Solder the joint, true the piece to shape in a collet block, and file the top and bottom faces (fig. 73). The stone should just fit into the top of the collet with the girdle (the largest diameter or length of a stone) just under flush. Now mark the position of the claws, in this case six of them, on the top face. With practice, this can be done by eye using a fine felt-tip pen. Half-way down the collet draw a line around and then mark in the shape of the cut-outs which form the claws. Ensure that the joint occurs between two of the claws (fig. 74).

Using a jeweller's saw, cut out the unwanted parts and finish by filing. Cut-outs are now filed into the bottom face in line with the claws and between the top cut-outs to about ¾ material thickness. While doing this either hold the collet between the fingers or push a headed nail through from the top and secure its point in a pin vice.

The cut-outs can be polished by rubbing the piece along a small hank of polishing threads dressed with tripoli.

The wire for the shank can be round, rectangular, half-round or square. Size it to the required diameter, leaving a gap just less than the diameter of the bottom of the collet between the ends. Now file the ends to a 90°V, angled back at the top and file V grooves on the bottom of the collet. This makes the assembly self-jigging for soldering.

Shank endings can be made in various ways, with plain, flattened, and flattened and divided ends. Some variations are shown in fig. 76.

Cut the seating for the stone into the inside face of the claw about 1 millimetre down. This can be done with an inverted cone burr, a stone seating burr of the correct size, a graver or a file. Make sure that you achieve a seating in which the stone sits well, i.e. square and stable, then, the stone removed, file the outside of each claw so it is round and tapered.

The whole ring can now be finish polished, then, holding the ring in a ring clamp, set well down and rested in the V of the bench pin, push the ends of the claws over the stone, alternating sides and using a pusher. Finally, burnish the claws smooth and snag-free.

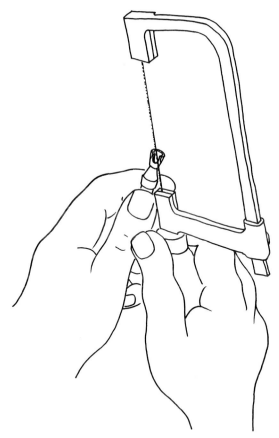

fig. 75
Sawing the top of a crown collet to form the claws.

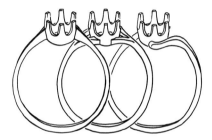

fig. 76
Variations on shank design.

7 Wood

Wood is an amazingly versatile material: solid or laminated, it can be shaped by sawing, drilling, carving, turning and bending. It can be coloured by natural wood dyes, coloured dyes or painted – choosing from a wide range of colours in gloss or matt paint.

Twigs and small branches can be used in constructing rustic or ethnic-style jewellery. Those woods with a natural hollow centre such as bamboo and elder simply require cutting to length to make tubular beads. Bark can either be left on and, once the wood has dried out, finished with varnish, or peeled off when the wood is green and the beads are stained and varnished later.

Wood surfaces can be inlaid with contrasting wood, silver and shell.

Plywood can be used as a support for foil and laminate constructions.

Plywood and thin solid wood is cut with a jeweller's saw on a bench pin. Small holes can be made with a normal twist drill. Holes much larger than 1 mm or 2 mm can be sawn out in thin wood or in thicker wood, drilled with a wood bit running at high speed. Solid wood can be lathe-turned using hand-held tools or on a small metal-turning lathe with a cross-slide mounted tool.

Edges and faces can be sanded to a clean face by rubbing the piece on a sheet of wet-and-dry paper resting on a hard smooth face, e.g. a sheet of plate glass. Curves can be shaped using half-round or round files and finished with a small piece of wet-and-dry paper wrapped around a short length of dowel.

Wooden components can be joined using traditional wood joints or simply butt-jointed using proprietary wood glues. (Using a stain finish on fabricated pieces is often best done before assembling with adhesive as the adhesive can impede the staining.) Balsa wood sold for modelling is easily cut with a craft knife and assembled with balsa cement. It can be sanded and painted with a wide range of gloss paint allowing the creation of complex shapes with a high gloss finish. Weighing little, it allows large, yet light, structural pieces to be built.

Plain wooden surfaces can be decorated by poker work. In this process a hot tool (originally, but not necessarily a poker) is used to burn the surface locally. Shaped stamps are used for repeated designs.

Where the grain of the wood is not to be part of the design, it must be filled and smoothed, which can be achieved after normal smoothing by filling the indentation with a proprietary wood filler and sanding. In the case of thin balsa wood, which can distort from the moisture in the filler, it may be better to cover it with thin tissue paper.

PROJECT 1

MULTI-COLOURED WOOD EARRINGS

Tools and Equipment

Junior hacksaw

Wet-and-dry paper

Round- and flat-nose pliers

Drill, drill bits, 0.8 mm and 3 mm

Round-nose pliers

Flat file

Side cutters

Materials

Hardwood (beech, ramin or similar)
6 mm thick

Dowel, about 3 mm diameter

Silver wire, 0.8 mm diameter,
half hard

Epoxy resin

Wood dye or paint, brush

Two heavy silver jump rings,
8 mm inside diameter

Method

Cut the bead components from solid wood. It is helpful to drill the hole for the dowel first or the face of the wood can be torn if a twist drill is used.

Mark out the shapes in pencil and cut them out with a junior hacksaw. File and sand the edges to shape. The edges of the holes should be bevelled. Make a cross-hole in the central dowel for the ear wires.

Paint, the pieces, assemble and glue them.

Twist open the jump rings, thread them through the dowel holes and twist them back, rotating them so that the joint is hidden inside the hole. This position can be maintained by use of a small amount of adhesive.

Make a loop in the thinner silver wire and thread it over the secured jump ring. Holding the loop, wrap the end of the wire around several times and cut it off square. Now form it into hooks and smooth the ends.

Multi-coloured wood earrings.

**fig. 77
Inlaid
hardwood
brooch.**

PROJECT 2
INLAID HARDWOOD BROOCH

Tools and Equipment

Hacksaw

Jeweller's saw and blades (size 1/0)

Round file, flat Swiss file

Fine and coarse wet-and-dry paper

Burnisher and pusher

Drill and small drill bit

Vice or bench hook

Materials

Selected piece of well-seasoned dark hardwood, e.g. rosewood

Silver or brass strips about 1 mm square

Epoxy resin

10 mm cabochon stone

10 mm collet

Wax polish

Commercial brooch pin unit

Method

Cut the piece of hardwood to size and sand the edges flat and square (most easily done by rubbing the wood on a sheet of wet-and-dry paper laid on a smooth flat face). Set the stone in the collet and polish the edges.

The lines and position of the stone are marked in pencil. Using a hacksaw and supporting the piece in a vice or on a bench hook, very carefully cut slots along the pencil lines. Drill a hole in the area of the stone and saw out the shape, finishing with a round file to give a good tight fit to the collet.

Now carefully file out the slots to take the silver or brass strips, allowing these to project slightly above the surface and beyond the edges of the brooch.

The strips are now cemented in place using epoxy resin. Gentle heat will hasten setting.

When the resin is set, saw the ends of the wires almost flush. Now sand the face and edges smooth, square and flat, finishing with very fine paper. The collet, set with the stone, can now be fixed in place with epoxy resin. The bezel should just project forward from the face of the wood.

Finally, fix the pin to the back with epoxy resin and give the wood a wax polish.

PROJECT 3

PIG BROOCH

Tools and Equipment

Bench pin

Jeweller's saw and blades (size 2/0)

Brush

Pencil and self-adhesive labels

Fine wet-and-dry emery paper

Drill and drill bit, 1.5 mm

Materials

Thin 3-ply plywood, about
    50×30 mm,
    1.5 mm thick

Wood glue

Paint of chosen colour

Commercial brooch pin unit

Epoxy resin

Method

Draw the pig on a label and fix it to the plywood. Drill or burn with a red-hot wire a hole in the centre of the tail and cut out the body. Now peel the label off carefully and use it to cut out the head. Again salvage the label and use it to cut out the nose, after first making the two holes for the nostrils.

Carefully sand away the rough edges and glue head to body and nose to head.

When the glue is dry, mark the position of the brooch pin. Then push three or four dressmaking pins into the back. Paint the back and edges, but not the brooch pin area, remembering that pigs need not always be pink. They can be any colour ... or striped or spotted! Now, holding the pins, paint the front and set the pig aside, propped on its pins, to dry. Finally, fix the brooch pin with epoxy resin.

fig. 78
Pig brooch.

8 Paper, Card and Foil

PAPER AND CARD

A low-cost and easily worked material, paper can be used to make substantial and colourful jewellery. The surface can be decorated with water-based paints and a durable finish given with varnish.

Two basic methods of construction are (1) folding, rolling and laminating cut pieces; (2) reducing the paper to an adhesive-bonded mash and moulding or laying up the shape. Folded or laminated constructions, being more delicate, are generally most suitable for earrings. Mash constructions are suited to bangles, and rolled constructions are used to make beads for necklaces or earrings.

Three-dimensional shapes can be formed using the origami (paper folding) techniques and are particularly suitable for earrings.

Tubes can easily be formed from paper rolled into spills. These can be cut and used in fabrications or flattened and woven into small mats, creating a three-dimensional surface.

Narrow strips of card glued on edge can be used to build up maze-like designs.

FOIL

Foil is produced both plain and paper-backed. Paper-backed foil has the advantage of being easily glued to paper, card and similar materials. For heavier sections, balsa wood provides an easy-to-fabricate structure for subsequent covering.

Paper-backed foil can also be stuck back to back to create a heavier double-sided sheet. Using heavy foil, a raised design can be created using a burnisher (see fig. 79).

fig. 79
Burnishing foil over a moulded base.

PROJECT 1

FOIL MOSAIC EARRINGS

Tools and Equipment

Craft knife   Cutting board   Leather punch

Materials

Paper-backed foil, 2 colours   Ear wires and large jump rings
Adhesive   Pin board (small sheet of insulation
Polystyrene strip (3×1 mm)   board or heavy cork mat)
Polystyrene cement   Pins

Method

Draw the design full-size on thin card and cut out.

Glue a small piece of paper-backed foil over the first area, overlapping the sides but with a straight edge along the dividing line with the next colour. Cut a piece of contrasting paper-backed foil to a wedge shape and glue it on to the card, butting up to the first piece. This process is repeated to complete the design.

Punch out holes with the leather punch and save the punchings.

It may be necessary to create additional punched pieces from scrap as not all the pieces can always be salvaged.

Now glue contrasting punched pieces in the holes and trim the overlapping foil to shape.

Make a second shape for the backing, and two matching pieces for the other earring.

Stick the pairs of cut shapes back to back and cut strips of thin polystyrene sheet longer than the foiled shapes but to the same width.

Set the first foiled shape on to the insulation board. Using pins to position it, bend a strip of polystyrene around and cement it to the edge, holding it to shape with pins. When dry, trim the ends and cement a strip along the other side which is trimmed to shape when dry.

Edge the second foiled shape in the same way. You can leave the polystyrene natural or paint it.

Make a small hole through the top corner, using a pin, and thread a large jump ring through (after twisting it open). Twist the jump ring closed and place a small dab of cement on the joint which you then position in the thickness of the card. Attach ear wires.

Foil mosaic earrings.

**fig. 80
Cross-section of
bangle showing
the layers of
card wrapped
with coarse
string prior to
covering.**

PROJECT 2
PAPIER-MÂCHÉ BANGLE

Tools and Equipment

Craft knife	Cutting board
Steel straight-edge	Bowl

Materials

Card	Wallpaper paste
Coarse string	Various coloured tissue paper
Glue	Varnish and brush
Newspaper	

Method

Wind a strip of thin card, 25 mm wide and about 1 metre long, round and round, gluing the faces, to give an inside diameter about 5 mm larger than the final size required.

When the glue is dry, wind a piece of coarse string around the centre of the outside (see cross-section in fig. 80) and glue it down.

Now mix wallpaper paste in a bowl and put small torn-up pieces of newspaper in to soak.

The shape is built up with the soaked pieces of newspaper, layer upon layer, until the desired section is achieved. Carry the layering around the inside to give a smooth contour. Now set the bangle aside to dry, which will probably take a few days.

The next step is to coat strips of tissue paper with paste and wind them around the bangle, creating the pattern. Some creasing can add to the textural effect. When it is fully dry, varnish the whole piece and hang it on a wire hook to dry.

PROJECT 3

COILED CARD EARRINGS

Tools and Equipment

Craft knife	Burnisher
Steel straight-edge	Fine wet-and-dry paper
Cutting board	Rule
Pin board and pins	Drawing pins
Pencil and paper	Greaseproof paper or tracing paper

Materials

Thin, good quality card	Ear wires
Glue	Jump rings
Aerosols of paint, two colours	

Method

Draw the design out full-size and pin the sheet to the pin board with drawing pins, covering it with greaseproof or tracing paper to protect it from glue.

Mark out parallel strips of card and cut to width (3–6 mm). (It is important to be accurate in keeping the width equal.)

Make the outline first. Hold a strip of card on a smooth clean surface and burnish the top face firmly, causing it to curl. Take up the curled strip and position it over the design, forming it to the exact shape. Mark the required length, cut the strip, and glue the ends together to form a frame.

Repeat this, positioning the shapes on the design, gluing the ends and holding them in place with pins, until you have built up the complete earring. Now repeat for the other earring.

When they are thoroughly dry, cut away any excess glue. Lay a sheet of fine wet-and-dry abrasive paper on a smooth surface and lightly rub each face of the pieces over to give a uniform thickness.

Now apply at least two coats of spray paint and allow to dry. You can give the edges a contrasting colour by spraying a piece of scrap card and placing the earrings on the card, removing them before the paint dries.

Finally, fit ear wires with jump rings.

**fig. 81
Design for
coiled card
earrings.**

9 Modelling Materials

Fired clay and porcelain have long been used in jewellery, often as an alternative to precious stones. A full range of colours, both in the material and with glazes, make them attractive materials, but a kiln is needed to fire the pieces, which introduces a slight complication.

An alternative is the use of a modelling material such as Fimo which can be hardened in a domestic oven and offers a wide range of colours.

Shapes are easily modelled after kneading by rolling, rolling out, cutting and modelling with simple tools. Colours can be kept separated or mixed to give marbled effects. Figures 82 and 83 show two methods of using modelling material.

Pieces produced by this method can be complete in themselves as, for example, beads, or they can be set in commercial or handmade settings.

The finished piece is not as hard or as resistant as ceramic, but is strong enough for most jewellery with the possible exception of rings.

**fig. 82
Making a mould by pouring plaster of Paris over a Plasticine master. The mould can be used to produce copies of the master in modelling material.**

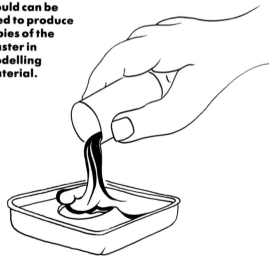

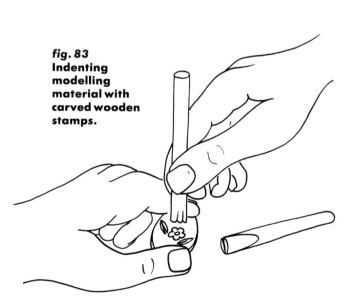

**fig. 83
Indenting modelling material with carved wooden stamps.**

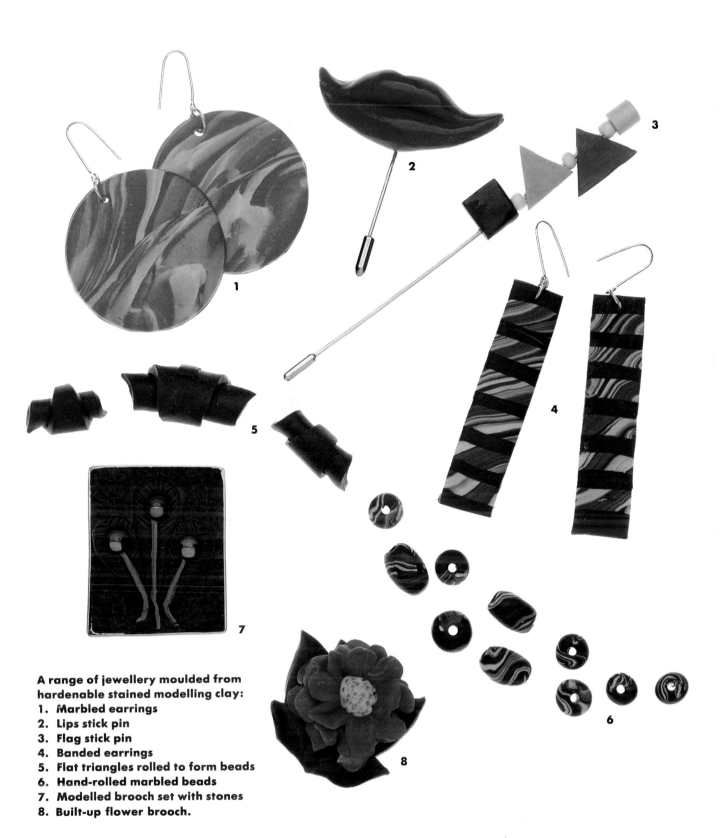

A range of jewellery moulded from
hardenable stained modelling clay:
1. Marbled earrings
2. Lips stick pin
3. Flag stick pin
4. Banded earrings
5. Flat triangles rolled to form beads
6. Hand-rolled marbled beads
7. Modelled brooch set with stones
8. Built-up flower brooch.

PROJECT 1

STRIPED EARRINGS

Tools and Equipment

Modelling board

Rolling pin

Plain kitchen knife

Modelling tool

Use of domestic oven

Materials

Hardenable stained modelling
   clay, e.g. Fimo

Fine wire

Fimo lacquer

Ear wires

Method

Roll out uniform sections, thick and thin, to suit the design, of contrasting colour Fimo. Cut these into 25 mm lengths and lay alternately side by side to form two squares, pressing the strips together.

Now roll them out flat and trim square.

Take a short length of thin wire, formed into a small loop and twist about three times. Splay the ends and trim to about 5 mm long.

Make an incision across the top corner of the square and insert the wire loop (fig. 84). Close the incision and smooth over the joint line with a modelling tool. Now bake the earrings at about 130°C for 20 to 30 minutes. (Instructions for baking are on the Fimo packaging; it is important to have the oven at the correct temperature.)

When the earrings are cool, lacquer them and fit the ear wires.

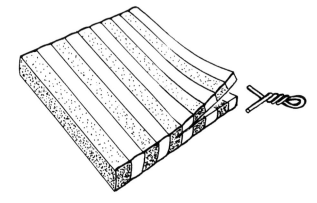

**fig. 84
Striped earrings; fitting a
wire loop into the corner.**

PROJECT 2

FLAG STICK PIN

Tools and Equipment

Modelling board   Darning needle
Rolling pin   Swiss file
Knife   Fine wet-and-dry paper

Materials

Hardenable stained modelling clay,   Fimo lacquer
  e.g. Fimo   Stainless steel wire or long hat pins
Glass beads   Pin cap finding
Epoxy resin

Method

Roll out small pieces of modelling material to about 3 mm thick, then cut out the various shapes with a knife and make a hole where the pin passes through.

Now bake the pieces and, when they are cool flatten the faces using the wet-and-dry paper. Inside shapes are finished with a Swiss file. Supporting each piece on fine wire, apply lacquer.

If you are making the pin from stainless steel wire, file a point at one end and polish it smooth on a polishing buff.

Now assemble the individual components on the pin, placing a dab of epoxy resin between them to keep them in place.

Finally, fit a commercial pin cap finding. See page 67, item 3 for colour picture.

fig. 85
Flag stick pin.

PROJECT 3

MODELLED BROOCH

Tools and Equipment

Modelling board   Rolling pin   Modelling tools

Materials

Hardenable stained modelling clay, e.g Fimo

Method

The design shown is just one example of a freely modelled piece. It is enhanced with mirror-backed glass cabochons each fixed in a pressed-in recess with epoxy resin.

The whole plaque is set in a silver frame completed with brooch findings. A colour picture of this project can be seen on page 67, item 7.

10 Glass and Enamel

Glass, coloured with metal oxides, has a well-established place in the history of jewellery from ancient times. Moulded, twisted, formed and fused glass can make complete pieces with the minimal use of normal findings.

Soda glass takes oxide colouring well and forms easily in a flame. A hot flame, such as can be achieved with propane and oxygen and reaching approximately 1,100°C is required. The torch head should be mounted on the work bench with the flame away from the operator. Purpose-made torches are available for hot glass work or metal cutting and if necessary you can adapt similar torches.

The piece is worked on the rod by initially making the end molten, twisting it continuously until a blob, the volume of the finished piece, is formed. This shape is easily formed using pliers and tweezers. Long shapes can be pulled out, formed and rejoined.

Colour can be introduced by dipping the hot glass into coloured glass chips or powder. This colour can be drawn through the piece or left on the edges.

Glass can be fused in an enamelling kiln. Cut pieces of coloured glass sheet laid on a sheet of mica or whiting, when fired in a kiln will melt and fuse together along the joints.

Glass reliefs can also be formed by firing a sheet so that it forms into or over a mould made from a material that can with withstand the high temperatures and coated with a chalk powder wash to prevent the glass sticking.

You can also pull strands of glass from a torch-melted pool of glass on a piece of fire brick using a simple poker. Such strands can be used to decorate glass pieces. Similarly, small glass beads can be fused into the basic piece as can both plain-coloured and millefiori pieces.

Highlights can be added with metal lustre enamels.

After a piece is complete it *must* be allowed to cool slowly to avoid stresses which can cause the piece to crack and fail. Leave it in the kiln after switching off, or keep it between two layers of ceramic fibre until it has cooled, which takes at least an hour.

Findings can be attached through formed holes or loops or fixed with epoxy resin.

Powdered glass coloured with metal oxides can be fused on to metal to produce an enamelled surface.

The enamel is best fused using an enamelling kiln (fig. 86) but simple

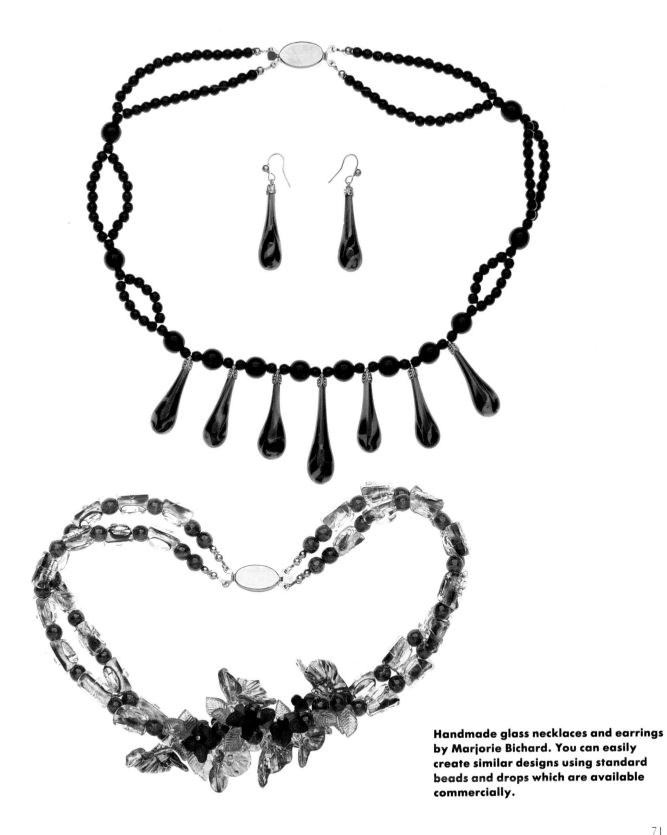

Handmade glass necklaces and earrings by Marjorie Bichard. You can easily create similar designs using standard beads and drops which are available commercially.

enamelling can be achieved by supporting the piece on a mesh-topped tripod and heating from underneath with a gas torch.

For simple enamelling, the metal shape – copper is suitable – is thoroughly cleaned, either with an abrasive pad or by heating to red heat and quenching in water. After cleaning, the metal must not be touched, so keep it in a shallow container of water and handle only with tweezers.

Dry the piece with kitchen paper and lay it on a clean, dry piece of paper. Brush the surface with a weak mixture of cellulose wallpaper paste or gum tragacanth and dust prepared enamel over it, creating a uniform layer, not too thick. After allowing the piece to dry, lift it into the kiln, preheated to about 850°C, and when it has fused to a glass surface, remove and allow to cool.

If the piece is fired by torch, the surface changes can be observed from granular, to orange peel, to gloss. Continuing the firing can cause the edges to burn and oxidize (sometimes done on purpose to achieve a decorative effect). Colours tend to darken when being fired and then lighten to their final shade on cooling.

The simplest form of decoration is trail enamelling, which gives a marbled effect. When dusting the metal surface with enamel add a small amount of contrasting colour. Once the enamel has fully fused, open the kiln door and drag an angled, pointed tool (a trailing poker) through both colours (fig. 87). The colours will stay separate but can be formed into whirls and scrolls.

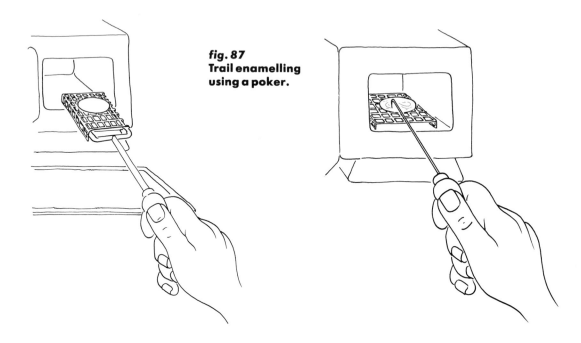

**fig. 86
Loading an
enamelling
kiln.**

**fig. 87
Trail enamelling
using a poker.**

It is possible to make a simple form of cloisonné enamelling in the following way. Make the main shape from copper sheet and cut it out some 3 mm to 4 mm larger than the finished piece. Form it up by lightly hammering the edges over a knocking-over plate that is the inside shape of the piece. Then make the top edge level by filing and rubbing it down on a sheet of wet-and-dry paper laid on a smooth surface. Finish polish the edges and then pickle and wash the piece.

Cut thin strips of copper as wide as the depth of the basic piece. Lay out the design of the cloisonné on paper and cut and form the pieces of the copper strip with pliers. These strips must be either curved or have a bend to help them stand on edge. Lay them in position in the piece to check the fit.

Now paint the inside of the piece with a very thin coat of cellulose wallpaper paste and dust with clear enamel flux. Handling them carefully with tweezers, place the pieces of strip in position, allow the paste to dry then fire the piece. The fused enamel will hold the strips in place and form the cloisonnés. The top edge needs to be finished smooth, washed and dried.

Then mix a slurry of enamel and water and load this into each cloisonné with a wooden toothpick. Take up excess water with a corner of blotting paper or paper towel.

After allowing the piece to dry, fire it. The process will probably need repeating until the cloisonnés are well filled.

Brooch pins or suspension rings can be soft-soldered on to complete the piece.

A form of champlevé enamelling can be made by piercing the design in a thick metal sheet of silver, gold or copper and soldering it with enamelling-temperature silver solder to a backing sheet. The resultant hollows can be enamel-filled and contrast with the plain metal surface.

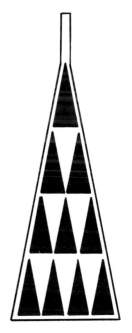

**fig. 88
Champlevé
pendant
design.**

PROJECT 1
CHAMPLEVÉ PENDANT

Tools and Equipment

Enamelling kiln
Mesh stand
Lifting tool
Enamel mixing pans –
　(watercolour mixing palettes are
　very good)
Watercolour brush
Wooden toothpicks or
　cocktail sticks
Kitchen paper
Heavy, flat file
Wet-and-dry paper

Materials

Silver or copper sheet, about
  1.5 mm thick (16 swg)
Enamel powder in the selected
  colours
Distilled water
  (tap water is just acceptable)

Silver steel rod for making
  punches 10 mm diameter, or
  acid etching equipment

Method

Saw and file the metal sheet to the outline shape and scribe the arrangement of
the triangular pattern on the face. The recesses to receive the enamel can either
be etched out with acid or punched in using a shaped steel punch. If the
punching method is chosen, the outside edges will require filing straight to
remove the distortion.

Make the front face level by rubbing the piece on a sheet of wet-and-dry
paper before polishing. To remove all traces of polish, pickle the piece in acid,
wash and dry. Three similar pieces are required for a set of earrings and
pendant.

The process of enamelling must be carried out in a clean area; an easy
expedient is to lay out a sheet of clean white paper on the work table.

Lift a small amount of enamel by spatula into one of the mixing pans and
drip in drops of distilled water, mixing with a cocktail stick into a smooth
paste. Tipping the pan will allow any excess water to drain.

Now with great care, start loading the cells with the paste, pressing it well
down and filling the space. Do not allow any of the mix to get on to the front
face.

Two silver champlevé pendants which were made using the same technique as that described in Project 1.

Repeat this process with the other colours for all the cells. Now put the piece to dry and switch on the kiln, raising it to about 800°C. This will drop to about 750°C when the door is opened, which is below the critical temperature of 779°C at which standard silver becomes unstable before melting at about 890°C. Transfer the piece on to the mesh tray and load it into the kiln. As soon as the enamel surface becomes smooth and shiny, about 1½ minutes, remove the piece from the kiln and set it aside to cool slowly. If any of the cells are not well filled, then repeat the process.

The surface of the enamel can be brought up to the level of the top of the piece or left in a concave shape.

When the enamelling is complete, the silver can be polished. This is best done by hand as machine buffing can contaminate the enamel.

Form over the top tab to enable the pieces to be mounted as earrings or pendant.

PROJECT 2
TRAIL-ENAMELLED BROOCH PLAQUE

Tools and Equipment

Enamelling kiln	Pickle bath and water
Mesh stand	Abrasive block or paper
Lifting tool	Absorbent paper towel
Trailing poker	Dropper
Enamel sieve	Watercolour brush
Mixing dishes	Toothpicks or cocktail sticks
Gas torch and hearth	

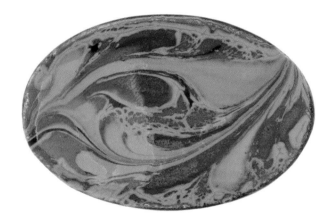

Trail-enamelled brooch plaque.

Materials

Enamels in various colours   Copper blank about 30×20 mm
Gum tragacanth or wallpaper paste

Method

The copper blank can be purchased or else made from copper sheet. It must first be cleaned free from oxides, grease, dirt and finger marks. This is achieved in one of two ways: either the blank is heated to a dull red heat and plunged into water, after which it must be dried on absorbent paper and handled only with a lifting spatula. Alternatively, the surface can be abraded with an abrasive block or paper and washed in clean water and dried. The enamelling process should start soon after to avoid oxidization of the surface.

Switch the kiln on now to save time.

Place the cleaned plaque, face up, on a clean sheet of white paper. Cleanliness is critical. Brush a very weak mixture of wallpaper paste or a gum solution over the surface and lift the piece (by spatula) on to a new sheet of clean paper.

Load prepared enamel of the background colour into the sieve and shake it over the plaque, giving a good uniform covering.

Now lift the plaque on to the mesh stand, using a spatula, and leave it to dry – conveniently on top of the kiln. This should only take a few minutes. When the kiln is up to temperature, lift the piece in with the lifting tool and close the door. You should be able to see the piece through a glass or spyhole but do beware of the effect of heat on the eyes.

The surface of the enamel will dull, form a characteristic orange peel surface and then turn uniformly smooth and shiny. The door can now be opened and the piece lifted out on its stand and left to cool slowly. Small dark flakes of copper oxide will fly from the back surface, so protect enamel, gum and work surface or these flakes may contaminate further work.

Put small amounts of the contrasting enamel colours in separate mixing dishes, drop in a small amount of water and mix to a stiff paste with a toothpick (a separate one for each colour to avoid contamination).

Place a lump of each colour at the centre or along the backbone of each intended swirl of the design, allow to dry, then load the piece into the kiln.

When the lumps start to collapse and go smooth, open the kiln door and, putting the tip of the trailing tool into the moulten lump, pull the design across the surface. Lift the poker clear at the end of each design. Practice will improve the technique! When swirling is complete, remove the piece and allow it to cool slowly. The edges can be cleaned of any excessive enamel by drawing them over a sheet of abrasive paper laid flat. The finished plaque can now be mounted as desired in a similar way to setting a cabochon stone.

PROJECT 3

FUSED GLASS PLAQUE FOR A BROOCH OR PENDANT

Tools and Equipment

Enamelling kiln   Whiting powder (chalk)

Kiln spatula   Glass cutter

Fire clay tile   Straight-edge

Materials

Selection of pieces of coloured glass sheet

Method

Lay the design on paper full size, remembering that the finished piece will be a little larger.

Using the glass cutter, cut the pieces of glass to size.

Mix whiting with a little water and spread evenly over the fire clay tile. When this is dry, assemble the cut pieces of glass on the tile, making sure all adjacent edges are touching.

Put the tile into the kiln and switch on. At about 900°C, near the melting temperature of the glass, the surface will become smooth and shiny. The contacting edges will unite and the outside edges go smooth. The kiln can now be switched off and the whole allowed to cool slowly to room temperature with the door shut. This time will depend on the type of kiln but will probably be about three hours.

In the example shown, the fused glass has been mounted like a cabochon stone in silver.

fig. 89
Fused glass plaque for brooch or pendant.

11 Feathers, Leather and Fabric

FEATHERS

Feathers, in natural colours or dyed, offer low-cost colour and texture for incorporation in jewellery. They are easy to cut and fabricate using a minimum of tools.

Structurally, a feather consists of a central tubular quill set on each side with barbs, which are linked by barbules to form a vane or web.

Naturally-moulted coloured feathers can be used with a minimum of trimming. Dyed feathers can be used similarly or cut and used in combination. Any cutting must take account of the lie of the barbs.

Being tubular, the quill can be used to make beads. The thinner part of the quill can, when stripped of the vane, be woven or plaited like straw.

Small panels of mosaic work can be made with cut webs, glued to a backing and set behind a window.

PROJECTS 1–5

Tools and Equipment

Straight-edge	Very sharp small craft knife
Cutting board	Pliers Snips

Materials

Selection of dyed and natural feathers

Fine silver wire   Glue   Beads

PROJECT 1

FEATHER NECKPIECE

Short lengths of cut feathers trimmed to within 5 mm of the quill are used to form this neckpiece. Use alternating or mixed coloured dyed feathers of similar quill size. Beads of glass, metal or plastic are used to space the feather beads and form a smooth moving joint. Use multi-strand beading thread for stringing, and terminate as described on pages 106–7.

**fig. 90
Feather neckpiece design using cut feathers and beads.**

PROJECT 2
TWO-COLOUR FEATHER EARRINGS

This design uses dyed turkey or goose feathers: you will need two of each colour and of a similar size. Trim the lower barbs well back to the quill; cut away the barbs and half of the quill on one side, taking care not to break the linking barbules. Using a minimum of adhesive, glue these barb pieces in place. When complete, cut the outline shape.

PROJECT 3
PEACOCK EARRINGS

Trim the tips of two small matched peacock feathers behind the eye pattern, as shown in the photograph. Wind a length of silver wire into a tube and form the end into a loop. This assembly can be glued in place with clear household glue, taking care not to get any glue over the barbs of the feather. Now fit a hook or ear wire to complete the pair of earrings.

Two-colour feather earrings.

PROJECT 4
MOSAIC PENDANT OR BROOCH

Mosaic patterns and pictures can be assembled by gluing the cut vanes of dyed feathers to a stiff card backing and setting them in a commercially produced or handmade 'glass'-fronted mount. Care is needed to achieve good gap-free fits between the pieces. You can also achieve contrast using only one colour by rotating the angle of the barbs in the shape. Mosaics like this can be glued to a stiff card backing and protected by a mount.

Pendant with a mosaic design which was constructed from pieces of dyed feather in a silver frame and mounted under a watch glass

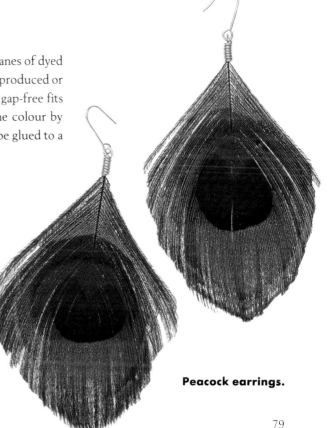

Peacock earrings.

PROJECT 5

QUILL EARRINGS

Pierce through the centre of some cut lengths of quill with a needle. A needle heated over a flame (hold it with pliers, if necessary) will pierce the quill without splitting it.

Put a small amount of adhesive between the quills at the centre and, working swiftly to complete the next stage before the glue dries, knot the ends of the thread and cut, leaving about 50 mm free at each end. Stick these down on a cutting board with tape, then cut the outside shape with a sharp craft knife. Rotate the pieces of quill to achieve the effect shown in fig. 91 and leave the piece to dry.

The assembly is finished with a single wire and beads as illustrated in fig. 91.

fig. 91
Quill earring design.

LEATHER

Thin leather can be used in a similar way to fabric and, conveniently, does not fray. It can be tooled with patterned punches before being fixed by adhesive to a backing. Cut sheet copper is very suitable for the latter.

Thick leather can be decorated by tooling. Holes can be punched for thonging and edges slit for fringing. The surface can be coloured by dying.

Studs in silver or plated metal can be easily fixed by tabs through cut slits.

Tooling of leather is done by punching with metal punches while resting the piece on a hard, smooth anvil. Specialist craft suppliers offer a range of such tools.

PROJECT 1

LEATHER HAIR SLIDE

Tools and Equipment

Cutting board   Decorative leather punches
Craft knife   and hammer
Leather punch

Materials

Piece of thick leather   Wooden dowel, 6 mm diameter

Method

This hair slide is simply made from one piece of thick leather. It requires two holes set about 50 mm apart and 8 mm in diameter. The shape around these holes can be as in fig. 92, or a simple rectangle, oval, circle or almost any other shape; the scope for decoration is limited only by the skill and imagination of the maker. I usually punch the design on this type of slide using smooth-ended punches and then dye the indentations. To complete the slide cut a wooden dowel to length and shape the ends with a pencil sharpener. Finish with wood dye and wax.

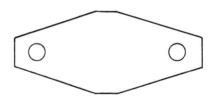

**fig. 92
Simple straight-sided pattern for leather hair slide.**

PROJECT 2

FRINGED LEATHER EARRINGS

Tools and Equipment

Cutting board   Round-nose pliers
Craft knife

Materials

Thin, coloured leather scraps   Silver wire

Method

Fringe a rectangle (40×60 mm) of thin, coloured leather by slitting with a craft knife for three-quarters of the 40 mm length about every 2 mm. Cut a single length of contrasting leather, 160 mm long and 2 mm wide. Knot the ends of this, fringe them, double the strip over and lay it at one end of the fringed piece with a 4 mm-long loop projecting at the top. Secure the strip in place with a small dab of adhesive and roll the fringed piece up. Again use a dab of adhesive to stick the end of the rectangle down and bind the top tightly with silver wire (see fig. 93). Fasten a heavy silver hook to the leather loop by a jump ring.

**fig. 93
Fringed leather earrings.**

PROJECT 3

LEATHER TASSEL BANGLE

Tools and Equipment

Cutting board   Craft knife   Leather punch

Materials

Thick leather sheet   Leather thongs   Beads
Scrap leather

Method

Construct this bangle from four panels of thick leather, with thongs each decorated with tassels to hold them together.

Make each rectangle 40×20 mm and punch the ends with four equally spaced holes. Tool and dye the design on the outer surface.

Join the ends of the panels by thonging with strips of contrasting leather (see fig. 94). Thread each thong into three beads and, finally, a tooled flower-shaped piece of leather, which is held in place with a single knot. Fringe the thong-ends that protrude beyond the knot.

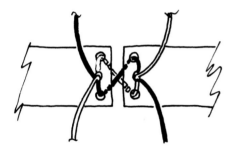

fig. 94
Knotting together the panels.

fig. 95
Leather tassel bangle with beaded thongs.

PROJECT 4

UMBRELLA BROOCH

Tools and Equipment

Cutting board
Craft knife
Round-nose pliers

Jeweller's saw and blade 2/0
Half-round Swiss file

Materials

Thin dyed leather
Copper sheet

Brooch finding
Epoxy resin

Method

Cut the outline from copper sheet about 1.5 mm thick. Smooth the edges and polish the whole piece. Then soft solder a bar pin to the back. Finish polish the handle and point on the front and make an indent near the very tip.

Cut out the umbrella body from the thin, coloured leather and stick it in place on the copper with epoxy resin. When the resin is dry, turn the piece over and cut out the rest of the umbrella shape with a craft knife, using the copper as a guide. Glue the leather down and tool on the 'folds' in the leather.

**fig. 96
Umbrella brooch.**

FABRIC

Plain-coloured felt, small-pattern printed cotton, small-pattern and plain silk can all be used to produce colourful, low-cost jewellery.

These materials can be made rigid very easily by fixing them to self-adhesive plastic sheet of the type sold for covering working surfaces.

Plain-coloured felt can be cut with scissors or a sharp craft knife and glued to a rigid backing, such as very thin painted plywood or styrene sheet. Because of the non-fraying quality of felt, complex mosaics can be made.

If the piece is to be three-dimensional, then coating the material with spray lacquer or brush varnishing it will produce a rigid structure.

Soft jewellery is made by cutting the material some 4 mm larger than the finished piece, placing right sides together and sewing 4 mm in from the edge, leaving a gap for turning inside out and stuffing. The gap is finished by hand sewing.

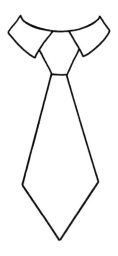

**fig. 97
Tie brooch.**

**fig. 98
Silk flower stick
pin.**

PROJECT 1

TIE BROOCH

Tools and Equipment

Cutting board   Craft knife   Scissors

Materials

Selected fabrics   Sheet polystyrene or card
Adhesives

Method

Cut the entire outline shape from sheet polystyrene or card, using a jeweller's saw or scissors. Smooth the edges with fine wet-and-dry paper or an abrasive block. Cut out the collar parts from fabric and fix in place with polystyrene adhesive, taking care not to mark the top faces.

Cut out a thin piece of polystyrene or card in the shape of the tie flap and glue on to it a piece of the chosen textile. Trim the cloth to within about 4 mm of the backing, slit it into the inside corners, fold it over and glue down.

Cover a piece of polystyrene or card in the shape of the knot in the same way. Glue the three pieces together, and glue a bar pin to the back.

PROJECT 2

SILK FLOWER STICK PIN

Tools and Equipment

Sheet metal-cutting tools   Soft soldering equipment

Materials

Sheet copper   Beads
Silk (plain, not patterned)   Epoxy resin

Method

Cut out the base piece of the pin from sheet copper and gently form it forward. Smooth the edges and soft solder the wire pins used to support the fabric flowers to the front (see fig. 99) and a long pin to the back. If the flower wires are formed in pairs with the joining piece bent at 90° (see fig. 100), they will stay upright during soldering.

Paint the piece front and back, leaving the pin unpainted. The easiest way to do this is to use car touch-up spray paint, first masking the main pin with a plastic drinking straw.

Now make the fabric flowers. To make the fabric more rigid, prevent it from fraying, and make it easier to mark out for cutting, stick it on to plain writing paper, on which you have drawn the flower shapes in ballpoint or with waterproof ink.

Use an even layer of clear general purpose adhesive and press the fabric on to the paper, eliminating any wrinkles. The line drawing will show through. Cut out the flowers, using scissors or a very sharp craft knife. For additional rigidity, you can cover both sides of the paper with fabric. The use of coloured papers enables a variety of colour effects to be achieved with fabric of a single colour. The flowers can be single, or multiple-layered. In the pin illustrated (fig. 98), the tiny flowers at the top of the pin were made with two small squares. Veins on the larger flowers were drawn on the backing paper. For mounting prick a centre hole in each flower with a needle.

When all the shapes have been cut out and formed, assemble them on to the projecting pins with a little adhesive and finish with a small coloured glass bead. Cut off the excess wire. A pin protector completes the project.

fig. 99
Stick pin base piece, showing location of pins.

PROJECT 3

STUFFED BOW BROOCH

Tools and Equipment

General sewing equipment

Materials

Scraps of coloured
    fine-patterned cloth

Brooch pin finding
Needle and cotton

fig. 100
The double pin.

Method

The making of this brooch employs normal dressmaking techniques. Make a paper pattern for each of the three rectangles that constitute the bow. Cut out the material, place right faces together and machine sew around for all but a short length through which the piece is turned right side out. When this is done, stuff each piece with foam or kapok and sew up the opening. Assemble the pieces by sewing them together at the back and attaching a brooch pin, again by sewing.

fig. 101
Stuffed bow brooch.

fig. 102
Stuffed bow brooch sewn on to a commercial brooch pin.

fig. 103
Twisted cord decorated with bead.

fig. 104
Twisted cord decorated with tassel.

fig. 105
Termination with jump ring twisted in.

12 Threads

Coloured threads can add a rich vibrance to jewellery. Silk and rayon have good shiny surfaces; cotton tends to be more matt.

Threads used to bind basic structures give colour and texture with the opportunity to bind on small beads and pendant pieces.

Threads can be twisted, plaited, woven or wound around a core.

A cord is easily produced by twisting and threads of many colours can be used. Decorative elements like beads (fig. 103) and tassels (fig. 104) can be incorporated into a cord.

Cords made by twisting can be made more interesting by randomly threading small beads on the threads prior to twisting. Short lengths of twisted threads can be bound with a contrasting colour and sheet metal beads can be crimped over the finished twist. Jump rings incorporated along the length can be used for suspending other decorative elements. There are a number of ways of attaching a jump ring to the end of a cord so that a fastening can be attached (figs 105–8).

Commercially-produced heavy cords can be used to hang pendants; tassels can be made into earrings. Cords, handmade or commercially-produced, can be plaited to make wider, flatter material and all the knots and twists of macramé can be utilized.

Short lengths of plastic tube coated with adhesive and bound with thread make attractive beads.

fig. 106
Free end of cord threaded through jump ring and then back through the twist.

fig. 107
Free end threaded through jump ring and then bound with thread.

fig. 108
Free end threaded through jump ring, knotted and then teased into a tassel.

Two necklaces made from twisted cord showing a plain design (above) and one which incorporates beads (below).

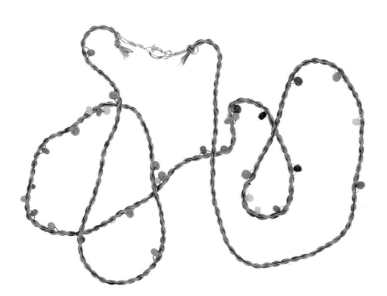

Twisted cord choker set with a handmade disc bead, two standard beads and two coiled wire beads.

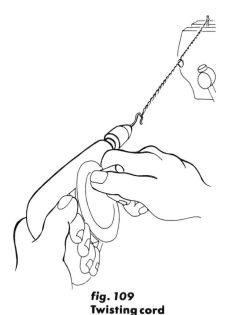

**fig. 109
Twisting cord**

PROJECT 1
MULTI-COLOURED TWISTED CORD NECKPIECE

Tools and equipment

Geared hand-drill

Cup hook or bent wire hook

Scissors

Fixed hook (wall-, bench- or
    vice-mounted)

Materials

Coloured threads

Beads

Solid jump rings

Open ring bolt rings

Method

Wind strands of thread about three times the length of the finished piece between a fixed hook and a drill-mounted hook (see fig. 109). Slide one solid jump ring over the hank when enough threads have been wound and the lengths have been (temporarily) tied off. Now twist the hank to the point when it noticeably shortens. Centralize the jump ring and hold it there with a wire hook. Keeping the cord under tension by pulling on the jump ring, bring the ends together (see fig. 110) allowing the threads to twist together. Remove the hook and cut the ends from the fixed hook and drill hook, threading a second jump ring over the free end. Bind it on with matching thread. Splay the cut ends out to form a small tassel, then fit a bolt ring, with open ring, to the jump ring.

Variation 1

This variation on the design has a central group of large beads threaded on after twisting. One way to make threading easy is as follows. Proceed to the point of twisting the two halves together but, before cutting the free ends, first coat the

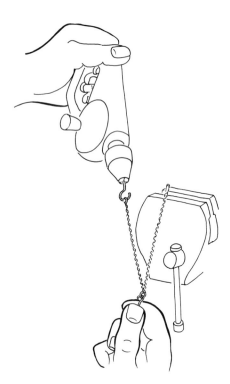

**fig. 110
Dividing the cord which self-twists.**

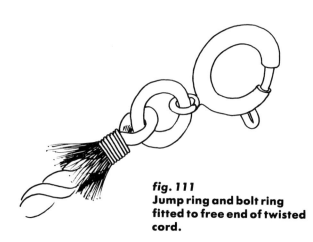

**fig. 111
Jump ring and bolt ring
fitted to free end of twisted
cord.**

last inch of cord with super glue and allow to dry. When cut through, this section will form a rigid threading 'needle' which can later be cut away and the end finished as in the original design. The central bead can be secured with a spot of glue, which will have the effect of holding the group central.

Variation 2
This necklace incorporates small beads all the way along its length. These are threaded along each individual thread, or pair of threads, prior to twisting. The beads can either be roughly spaced equally along the threads or concentrated to the middle of each half to give a concentration at the centre front of the finished piece. Otherwise proceed as in the original design.

PROJECT 2

THREAD AND BEAD BANGLE

Tools and Equipment

Cutting pliers	Hand-drill
Soldering iron	Craft knife
Sewing needle	

Materials

Salvaged electrical copper wire	Jeweller's saw, blades and
Solder	bench pin
Coloured thread	Narrow bandage
Beads and dangles	Super glue

Method

Make the core of several 350 mm long strands of copper wire (enough to finish with a 4 mm diameter). Twist the core by holding one set of ends in a vice and fixing the other in a drill chuck. The twist should be uniform. Remove the core from the drill and vice, bend it by hand into a ring about 5 mm larger than the finished inside size of the bangle. Cut the ends square and soft solder the joint.

Cover the core neatly with a layer of bandage using glue to secure the ends.

Twist together lengths of coloured thread, as in Project 1, to form a thick, multi-coloured cord about 2 mm diameter.

Bond one end of the cord with super glue and cut square. Attach this (again with super glue) to a point on the inside of the wire core on the centre line. Holding the end in place, wind the cord around the core, finishing off by bonding the end and attaching it to the wire core with super glue.

Bind over the joint and at other places around the bangle with thread of a contrasting colour, and sew small beads and dangles to these bindings.

**fig. 112
Thread and
bead bangle.**

**fig. 113
Tassel earring.**

PROJECT 3

TASSEL EARRINGS

Tools and Equipment

Scissors   Pliers

Materials

Coloured threads   Solid jump rings
Beads   Fine silver wire
Ear wires   Card

Method

Cut a piece of card about 80 mm wide. Wind the thread round and round over a width of no more than 5 mm. When sufficient thickness is built up, tie a temporary thread at one end, holding the threads together. Cut through the opposite end. Feed the bound end through a solid jump ring and then pull the cut ends through the loop and pull tight. Bind the threads with matching or contrasting thread. The temporary binding can be cut away and the ends of the tassel cut to the required length. Form a hook in the end of a wire and fit it over the jump ring. Thread beads on and form the end into a loop. Fit the ear wire and repeat with the matching earring.

13 Shell

Shells, whole and carved, have long been used in jewellery. Drilled with a small hole they make instant beads. The helmet shell (mother-of-pearl) has been traditionally carved into cameos or cut into flat sheets, which are pierced or engraved for individual pieces or as insets in other materials.

Shell is best worked with carbide tipped tools, but for the home jeweller, normal saw blades, files and cutting burrs can be used. However, they will become more quickly worn than when used for cutting metals.

These items of jewellery show the different effects which can be created from shell. The necklace (above) was made from drilled baroque shell pendant beads and round shell beads. The earrings (right) are simply two discs of paua shell with a hole drilled for ear wires.

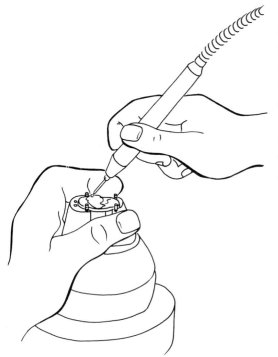

Thicker shell can be carved and is easily cut by a burr in a pendant drill (see fig. 114). The shell can be held in an engraver's block. Establish your design on paper, then transfer it to the shell using a fibre pen. Cut away the basic depths and finish the design using files, wet-and-dry paper and progressively finer cutting media (e.g. carborundum), finishing with tin oxide made into a paste and worked with short lengths of split wood or bamboo.

Thin shell plaques can be pierced with a drill and cut with a jeweller's saw. Coloured awabi and paua shell is commonly available in oval and circular discs, which can be lightly carved, pierced and engraved. Flat shell beads and heishi are available commercially.

fig. 114
Carving shell which is held in an engraver's block.

PROJECT 1

ABALONE, PAUA SHELL
OR MOTHER-OF-PEARL EARRINGS

Tools and Equipment

Jeweller's saw, blades (size 2/0), bench pin	Half-round Swiss file
Hand drill and small drill bit	Fine wet-and-dry paper
	Pliers

Materials

Flat shell	Ear wires	Jump rings

Method

Work out the design of the cut-out on paper and transfer it on to a self-adhesive label. Carefully position this on to the shell and drill small holes in the cut-out areas. These can now be removed, using a jeweller's saw, and any imperfections corrected by filing.

Attach each piece by a jump ring on to an ear wire.

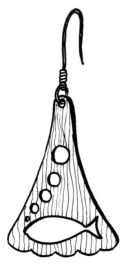

fig. 115
Design for pierced shell earring.

PROJECT 2

BAROQUE SHELL NECKLACE

Tools and Equipment

1.5 mm high-speed twist drill

Anvil and small piece of hardboard

Circular cutting punches

Dome punches and dome block

Flat-end 1.5 mm punch

Polishing equipment for metal

Round-nose pliers

Flat-nose pliers

Side cutters

Materials

Baroque tumbled shell pieces

Silver soldering equipment

Shell beads

Silver wire 0.8 mm diameter

Silver sheet 0.5 mm thick (25 swg)

Silver chain 18/18 Trace

Bolt ring and jump ring

Method

The design is established primarily by selection of the pieces of shell that make up each segment. It is helpful, when designing, to set the groups of shell out on a sheet of paper, using Plasticine to hold them upright and drawing in the linking elements. Mark the thread line on each piece of shell and drill a hole through.

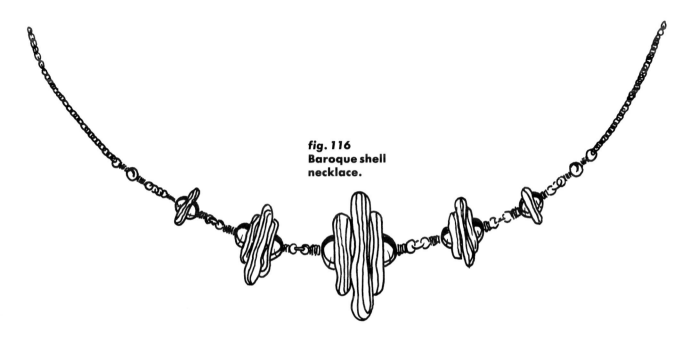

**fig. 116
Baroque shell
necklace.**

Now cut silver half cups from sheet, using circular cutting punches on a piece of hardboard resting on an anvil. Progressively smaller discs are used, dependent on the sizes of the shell. Use dome punches to shape the cups. The hole required in the centre of each domed cup is most easily made with a sharp-edged, flat-ended punch. The cups rest on a piece of hardboard on the anvil and the holes are punched outwards. Any burrs can be filed off and the outside of the cups polished. (It is helpful to thread each cup on a piece of wire to make it easy to hold against the polishing wheel.)

The jump rings joining the segments can be soldered closed and finished by polishing.

Leaving about 20 mm free at either end of each section, form a loop in the silver wire and slide on a solid jump ring. Then wind the wire around three times and cut off cleanly. Thread on the cups and shell pieces and, leaving just enough space for three turns, make a loop in the other end of the wire. Thread on a solid jump ring, complete the loop and wind the wire around, as before, cutting it off flush.

Repeat the process for the other assemblies, finishing off with short lengths of chain, one ending in a bolt ring the other in a jump ring.

PROJECT 3

MOSAIC SHELL BROOCH

Tools and Equipment

Bench pin

Vice

Jeweller's saw and blades

Soldering iron

Coarse and fine wet-and-dry paper

File

Tin oxide polishing compound

   and a piece of hard felt

Materials

Mixed shell pieces, abalone, paua

   and mother-of-pearl

Epoxy resin

Brooch findings

Copper sheet

Steel sheet

Soft solder

4 mm thick mild steel for

   forming tool

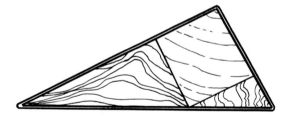

fig. 117
Mosaic shell brooch.

Method

Saw and file the piece of steel to the inside shape of the brooch and cut the copper sheet some 6 mm larger all round. Clamp both together in a vice and hammer over the edges of the copper. Rubbing the edges on wet-and-dry paper resting on a flat, hard surface will produce sharp edges. The pin assembly is now soft soldered to the back. Lay out the design on paper and transfer each part to a self-adhesive label. Place these on the shell and cut out the desired pieces by sawing and filing.

Dry assemble all the pieces, correcting any imperfections. Now mix the epoxy resin and, with the brooch supported in a slot made in a piece of wood, glue the pieces in place. Then cure in a domestic oven for about 30 minutes at 75°C.

Rub the front face flat on wet-and-dry paper (see fig. 118) and finish polish, using wet felt and tin oxide. Rubbing the piece over the felt held flat on a smooth face will prevent excessive rounding of the edges.

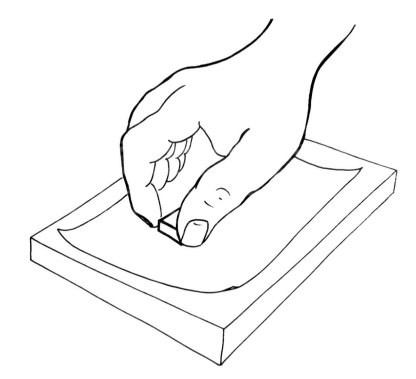

**fig. 118
Smoothing a
shell mosaic on
a sheet of wet-
and-dry paper.**

14 Plastics and Resins

The family of plastics probably offers the most exciting range of materials available to the jeweller today. Plastics fall into various groups, each with particular characteristics and applications for jewellery.

THERMO-PLASTICS

This group includes **polystyrene** and **ABS**, produced in thin sheet, rod, tube and other sections. Both are available from model-making shops and can easily be cut with a craft knife or fine jeweller's saw. Heat from a hair dryer or domestic oven will soften the plastic for bending and it is easily joined with polystyrene cement. (N.B. *Care is needed when heat forming as this material is flammable and will ignite in contact with a flame.*) Although made in a wide range of colours these plastics are often available only in black or white. They can be painted with the type of paint used by model-makers.

Perspex (or **plexiglass**) is also a thermo-plastic material, produced in a very wide range of colours both solid, transparent, translucent and opalescent. Available in sheet, rod, tube and cross-sections of various shapes, it can be cut and polished with hand tools. The colours go right through the material and edges can be polished.

Acetate, in film and thin sheet, can be clear or coloured. It is easily cut with a craft knife or scissors and holes can be cut with punches.

It is easily softened by heat and can be formed by being draped over a simple former or, for more defined shapes, by means of vacuum (see page 97).

Flexible plastic, such as **PVC** (sheet and tube) is available in a wide range of sizes and colours. Small-size tube, referred to as sleeving, is sold through electrical/electricians' materials suppliers for insulating conductors.

PVC is easily cut with a craft knife, cutting punches and scissors. The sheet can be folded and twisted. The sleeving can be threaded over wire to make it rigid and with short lengths fitted end to end will give bands of colour.

Some sleeving is heat-sensitive and will shrink on to a core when heated.

THERMO-SETTING LAMINATES

Typically sold under such names as Formica and Wareite, for surfacing work tops, it is generally only available in thin sheet and is not suitable for forming.

Offcuts are frequently available in a range of patterns and colours from hardware shops. The coloured face is hard and smooth but the back face is lightly textured and dull brown in colour. This disadvantage is overcome by gluing pieces back to back, using impact adhesive.

POLYESTER AND EPOXY RESINS

Two-part resins allow shapes to be cast in clear, tinted or coloured resin. Different ratios of hardeners, accelerators and dyes are used, so follow the manufacturer's instructions closely.

Moulds can be made from almost any material which can be finished to a super-smooth surface (e.g. hard wood) and then coated with wax or silicon to act as a release agent.

VACUUM-FORMING ACETATE SHEET

Simple vacuum-forming allows the creation of three-dimensional, multi-curved shapes in sheet acetate.

A simple vacuum box (see fig. 119) is easily made from a redundant confectionery, or similar, tin and lid. Drill a hole in the side of the tin and insert a cycle inner tube connector. Soft solder it in place. Drill or punch a pattern of holes in the lid and soft solder the lid down to make a sealed container. Make a simple double frame out of strips of wood to the size of the tin, and stick self-adhesive foam sealing strips on the top and bottom faces of the lower frame and around the top of the box. The whole assembly, tin and frame, is held together with heavy rubber bands.

Use a normal cycle pump to produce the necessary low pressure within the tin by reversing the piston washer inside. Pulling on the pump will thus reduce the pressure in the box.

The pattern (shape) over which the acetate is to be formed can be made from almost any hard, smooth-finished material (e.g. plywood or hardboard). It should be built up high enough to just touch the face of the material being formed.

The acetate sheet is laid between the two frames and this is held on to the lid of the tin with rubber bands and warmed with a hair dryer. When the sheet becomes pliable pull out the pump handle. (It can be useful to fix the body of the pump to the work top so it can be used single-handed.) The sheet will form down over the pattern. When cool, it can be removed and trimmed to shape.

For deeper forming, heavier equipment can be built which will form styrene sheet into large rigid shapes.

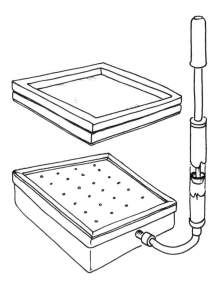

fig. 119
Vacuum box and pump.

fig. 120
Pattern modelled in
Plasticine on a ceramic tile.

fig. 121
Plaster of Paris mould cast.

RESIN CASTING

Small intricate solid shapes with one flat face can be cast in resin. To make a simple one-piece mould, a pattern of the required shape is modelled in Plasticine set on a hard working surface, such as a piece of glass or laminate (see fig. 120). Surround the model with a wall of plasticine about twice the height of the model with at least a 20 mm gap around it (fig. 121). This space is filled with a smooth mixture of Plaster of Paris. When fully hard and dry, the plasticine wall and model are removed. The dry mould (fig. 122) is now waxed in the hollow and on the top face. Resin can now be mixed according to the maker's instructions, slowly and carefully poured into the waxed cavity and allowed to harden. Attachment findings can be set in the resin before it hardens.

fig. 122
Resin shape cast in plaster
mould. The cast in support
ring is held in place with a
matchstick while the resin
hardens.

PROJECT 1
LAMINATE SHEET EARRINGS

Tools and Equipment

Jeweller's saw and blades (2/0)   Hand drill and 1 mm drill bit
Half-round Swiss file   Pliers

Materials

Laminate off-cuts – the thinner   Laminate adhesive
  of the commercially available   Earring findings
  laminate is best   Jump rings

Method

Lay out the design on paper and transfer the complete design and each colour area separately to self-adhesive labels.

Lay these on the laminate and cut out (a) the entire shape, (b) the two inner shapes, in contrasting colours, ensuring a good fit on touching edges. The single piece forms the back.

fig. 123
Laminate sheet
earrings.

Spread the laminate with adhesive and glue pieces of each colour back to back.

Trim the outside shape. Drill the hole and finish the edges, making them smooth and burr free.

Attach the ear wires and the earrings are complete.

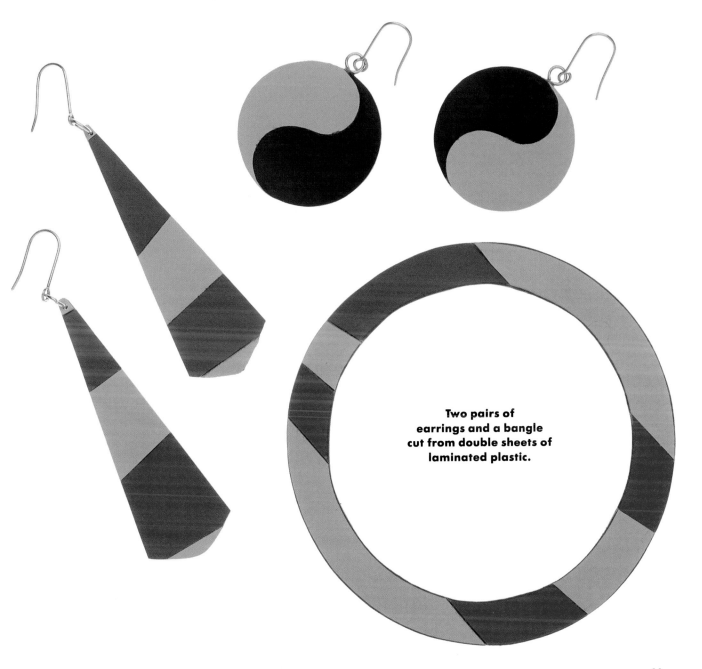

Two pairs of earrings and a bangle cut from double sheets of laminated plastic.

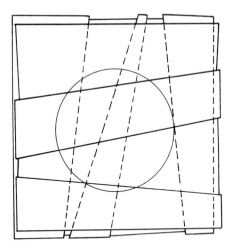

**fig. 124
Front and back
layout of
alternately
coloured
laminate.**

PROJECT 2

LAMINATED BANGLE

Tools and Equipment

Jeweller's saw and blades
(size 2/0)

Half-round Swiss file
Fine wet-and-dry abrasive paper

Materials

Laminate off-cuts

Laminate adhesive

Method

Lay out the design in full and transfer the shapes of each individual segment to a self-adhesive label. Now affix this to the laminate sheet, allowing spare material on all but the butting edges.

Cut out the pieces but only finish the butting edges, leaving free material on all the others.

Repeat for the other side, making sure that joint lines cross and do not coincide.

Now using a small amount of adhesive, join the edges of each side together. When these are dry, glue both halves together and allow to dry.

The outline and inside can now be cut to the finished shape and made smooth.

Many variations on this theme are possible, with square, octagonal, oval or triangular outside shapes.

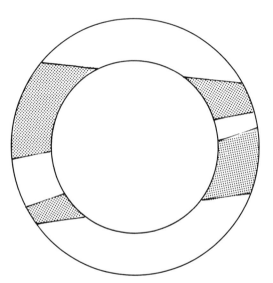

**fig. 125
Finished
bangle.**

PROJECT 3

VACUUM-FORMED ACETATE EARRINGS

Tools and Equipment

Home-made vacuum-forming equipment and heat source (see page 97)
Pliers

Materials

Acetate sheet   Ear wires
Model-makers' paint   Silver wire
Paint brush   Polystyrene cement

Method

A simple half-pattern is made, using wood or any similar hard, heat resistant
material. The design must be symmetrical, otherwise accurate left- and right-
hand patterns are required.

Four mouldings are taken, and the skirt part is cut away. This is easily and
accurately achieved by firmly holding a craft knife on a suitable block of wood
and with the formed sheet supported on the pattern, rotating it across the
blade of the craft knife.

Two halves are held together and a mark made at the centre top. A small V
cut is made in each half.

A twisted wire loop is made for each earring with splayed ends and the two
sides are glued together, trapping the wire loop.

When dry, the pieces can be painted in plain colours or decorated as
required and ear wires fitted.

**fig. 126
Vacuum-formed
acetate earrings.**

PROJECT 4

HOOP EARRINGS

Tools and Equipment

Pliers – cutting and forming   Craft knife

Materials

Steel piano wire   Ear wires
PVC sleeving   Adhesive
Large hole beads   Short length of silver wire

Method

Slide the PVC sleeving over cut lengths of the steel wire and form round into circles with an overlap of 5 mm. Remove the sleeving from each end for 5 mm and slip a bead over. Form the ends of the wire into two hooks and clinch them together. Slide the bead over the joint and secure with a little adhesive. Make four hoops in the two sizes. Cut a small V-shaped nick on the inside of each hoop, opposite the bead; it helps position the loop.

Form a figure of eight with a small and large loop (see fig. 127) from the silver wire, one for each earring, and use this to join the hoops. Finally, add ear wires.

fig. 127
Hoop earring.

15 Stringing Beads and Making Chains

BEAD STRINGING

Bead stringing is one of the most ancient of the jewellery crafts and forms a suitable introduction to jewellery making. Little is needed by way of tools and equipment and, with a little skill and imagination, original and attractive pieces are easily made.

Almost any small item with a through-hole or in which a hole can be made is suitable for stringing, although it is suggested that commercially available

A selection of commercially available beads, with manmade beads on the left and some made from semi-precious stones on the right.

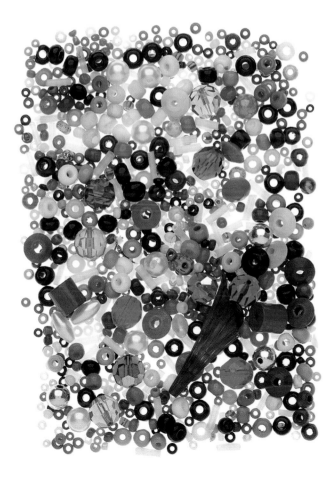

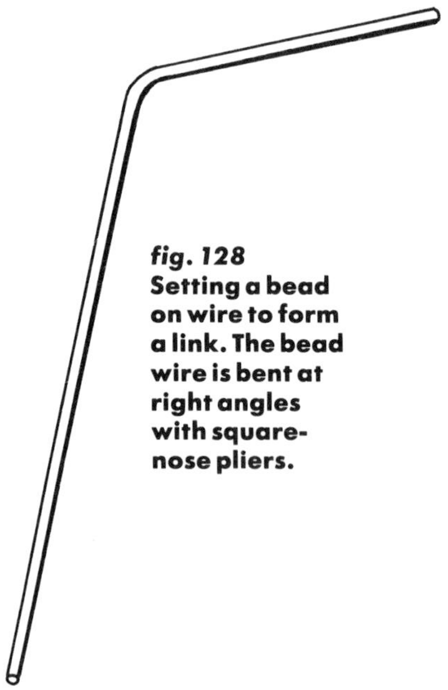

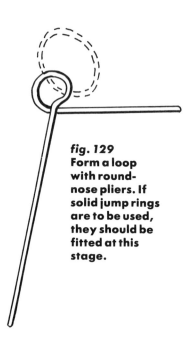

**fig. 128
Setting a bead
on wire to form
a link. The bead
wire is bent at
right angles
with square-
nose pliers.**

beads should be used initially. These can be purchased in a wide range of materials: natural stones, pearls, coral, wood, brass, glass and plastic, to name just a few.

Once the basic threading and knotting techniques have been mastered, the design scope is limitless.

The most common piece of strung bead work is the necklace, but earrings, brooches and bangles can also be made by stringing.

The basic components are beads, string, terminations and fastenings.

Strings Silk bead cord is very strong, knots easily and is available in a range of colours to match or contrast with the beads.

Multi-strand nylon is similar to silk, can stretch a little more, but is less liable to fray and does not rot. Both silk and nylon are available in a range of thicknesses, sized 1 to 10, and the general rule is to use the thickest one which will easily pass through all of the beads. Coloured threads are available to match or contrast with the beads.

A word of warning. Some stone beads are drilled through from both sides and do not always line up exactly. With care, a diamond drill, well wetted, can be used to smooth the junction and make the bead easier to thread. Undue force is liable to crack the bead.

For stringing heavy beads, beads with sharp edges or for stringing a heavily loaded piece, tigertail is used. This is a fine twisted wire coated with plastic. Its

**fig. 129
Form a loop
with round-
nose pliers. If
solid jump rings
are to be used,
they should be
fitted at this
stage.**

**fig. 130
Holding the loop with flat-
nose pliers, wind the 'tail'
around the main wire and
snip off the end.**

disadvantage is that it is more rigid and a delicate string of beads will tend to be stiff and not hang well.

Monofilament nylon is a clear semi-rigid line similar to fishing line. It is not easy to tie and is quite rigid even when thin.

For heavy ethnic style pieces, leather thongs can be used, with the leather itself being a visible part of the design. Twisted coloured cords can be used in a similar way.

Beads may be threaded on to thin wire when a rigid assembly is required, as with pendent earrings or the centre-piece for a choker (see figs 128–33). Wire pins with a head or loop end can be used to make pendant earrings.

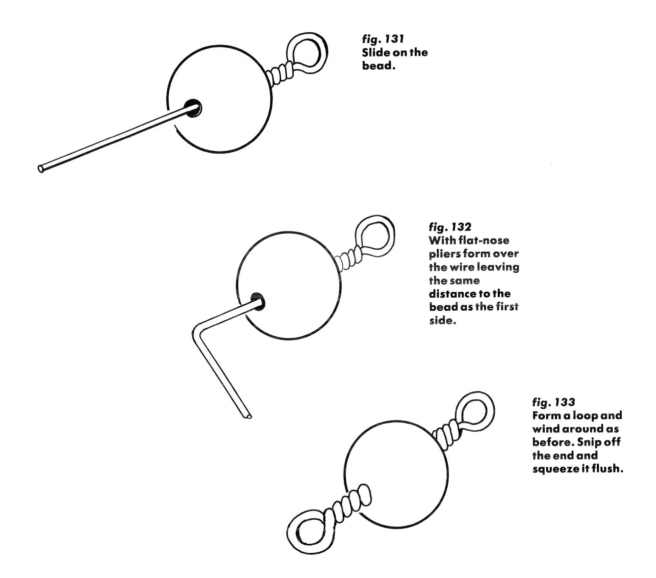

fig. 131
Slide on the bead.

fig. 132
With flat-nose pliers form over the wire leaving the same distance to the bead as the first side.

fig. 133
Form a loop and wind around as before. Snip off the end and squeeze it flush.

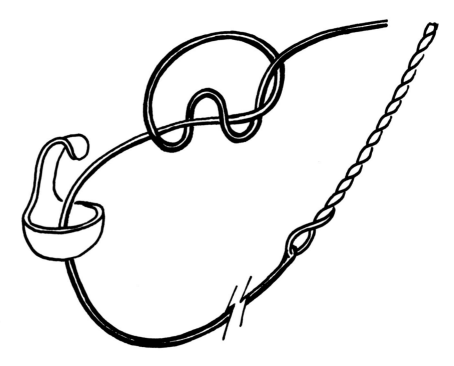

**fig. 134
Knot for a bead
tip showing the
threading
needle.**

**fig. 135
The bead tip can
be tied off by
dividing the
cord and
making two
knots to form a
reef knot.**

Threading The traditional threading needle is made from a length of fine twisted wire which may be already fitted to the thread or can be purchased separately. They are easy to make from fine copper wire.

You can also coat multi-stranded threads lightly in super glue to make a rigid end, suitable for threading. Before stringing you will need to knot on the bead tip (fig. 134).

Terminations The ends of a string of beads usually terminate in a fastening: either a bolt ring and jump ring, or a barrel fastening.

The fastening may be bound and knotted directly to the string. In this arrangement, the string can be covered with bouillon or French wire to protect it from wear. This is a spring-like wire, which is cut to length and threaded over the end of the string before knotting.

A simpler termination is to use bead tips. These are small cup like findings with a hook. The end of the string is threaded through, knotted with a reef knot and pulled tight into the cup (see fig. 135). A small dob of adhesive will prevent the knot moving. The hook can now be bent around the fastening hook or ring.

Knotting   Knots are used for attaching fastenings and bead tips. They can also be made between the beads. This has the double advantage of spacing the beads and in the event of a broken string, preventing all of the beads sliding off.

The technique of between-bead knotting is to use knotting tweezers or a needle in the knot (see fig. 136), thus preventing it tightening until it is hard up against the bead. The last two spacing knots are omitted and after being double looped around the jump ring or bolt ring, the string is threaded back through the end bead, knotted (see fig. 137), then through the second bead and knotted. After passing through the third bead the string is cut.

An alternative to knotting is to use crimps. These are like small metal beads which can be compressed on to a doubled string.

Design and selection   Beads can be laid out on bead boards in the process of selection and arrangement. These are grooved boards which help keep the beads together. A simple alternative is a triple folded piece of card in a shoe box lid.

Basic tools for stringing beads

Bead board	Pliers
Knotting tweezers with rounded points	Scissors
	Craft knife
Needles	Rule or tape

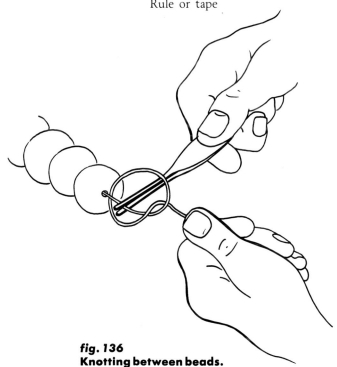

**fig. 136
Knotting between beads.**

**fig. 137
Stringing beads with knots between the beads. The last two beads are left unknotted. The needle takes the string twice around the jump ring back through the beads, knotting after each one.**

MAKING CHAINS

Many varieties of chain can be purchased ready-made in standard sizes. You can either purchase basic chain in long lengths, cutting it as required, or make up basic chain from wire section or sheet. Silver wire is a good material from which to start chain making. If over, say, 70 cm (28 in), chains can be a continuous length as they will easily slip over the wearer's head. Shorter chains require a fastening. Bolt rings, barrel clasps and hooks are typical fastening arrangements.

TYPES OF CHAIN TO MAKE

Trace chain (fig. 138)   This is the most basic chain, consisting of round or oval links made from round wire. If the wire is thick (greater than one third the inside diameter of the ring) the links can be strong enough without soldering the joint.

Belcher chain (fig. 139)   Similar to trace chain, it is made from oval links of oval cross-section.

Box chain (fig. 140)   Similar again to a trace or belcher chain, but made from flat sheet or strips. Each link is made into a square shape the inside dimension being just a little more than the width of the strip. The solder joint is hidden by the next link.

**fig. 138
Trace chain.**

**fig. 139
Belcher chain.**

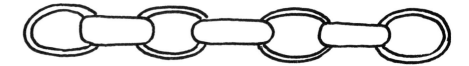

**fig. 140
Box chain.**

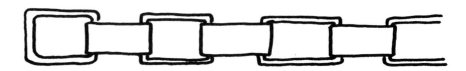

Curb chain (fig. 141)   This is made like trace chain with soldered links. It is then twisted so that it lies flat.

Loop-in-loop chain (fig. 142)   All the individual loops are made separately and the joints soldered. Each loop is elongated and then folded over, making two pairs of loops at right angles.

These are threaded through each other and a chain built up. The assembly can be rolled or drawn to make a snake chain.

Bar link chain (fig. 143)   Bar chains offer wide scope for individual design. The basic design is a bar at the ends of which are rings for joining by jump rings to the next bar. The construction of the bar may be from a single piece of section, twisted, open wires or any other appropriate fabrication. Flexibility and variety are improved by joining the bars with short lengths of loop chain.

Composite chains   Interest and variety can be achieved by building up a chain from short (e.g. 2 cm) lengths of machine or handmade chain.

**fig. 141
Curb chain.**

**fig. 142
Loop-in-loop
chain.**

**fig. 143
Bar link chain.**

PROJECT 1

TAPERED TRACE CHAIN

Tools and Equipment

Bench pin

Chain link triblet

Jeweller's saw and blades
(size 3/0 or 4/0)

Hard soldering equipment

Pliers

Length of 4 mm-diameter metal rod

Polishing equipment

Materials

Annealed round silver wire –
0.6 mm (23 swg) or 0.8 mm
(21 swg) diameter

Bolt ring

Silver solder

Method

The chain link triblet is a round section tapered piece of steel. At its largest diameter it is 20 mm, tapering to 4 mm at the small end. The length of the taper is 30 mm with a parallel portion at each end. Ideally, this tool is turned on a lathe. If this is not possible, then it can be improvised from some manufactured component with similar dimensions.

The wire for forming the links must be annealed to make it less springy and easy to bend.

To form the links, a length of wire is held along the small diameter portion of the triblet and the wire wound around, maintaining an even tension and keeping the coils touching.

When enough turns have been made for half the chain, a second coil is wound. Cut off the free ends.

Now with the coiled wire cone resting on the bench pin and firmly held, cut off successive rings, one at a time, and lay them out in a straight line to keep the sequence.

Wind a length of wire on the 4 mm rod and, similarly cut it into jump rings.

Still keeping the size sequence, twist the taper-wound rings flat with the ends butting. Solder the joints using very little solder.

Starting with the smallest of one set, join the soldered rings with the jump rings. When the largest ring is reached, the other group of soldered rings is joined, starting at the largest.

When the whole chain is assembled, the small joining rings are soldered. Fig. 144 (page 110) shows how the soldered joint is laid to minimize the chance of affecting existing soldered joints.

After pickling, the piece is polished. To help prevent the chain becoming entangled with the buffing wheel, it is held stretched over a short length of wood. Attachment of the bolt ring completes the piece.

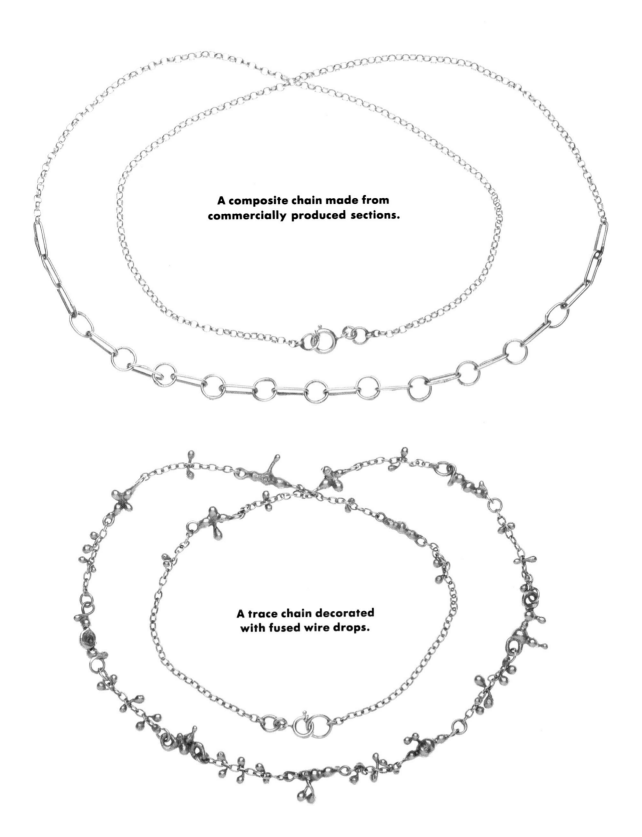

A composite chain made from
commercially produced sections.

A trace chain decorated
with fused wire drops.

PROJECT 2

BAR LINK CHAIN

Tools and Equipment

Jeweller's saw and blades (size 2/0)   Polishing equipment
Hard soldering equipment   Metal rod, 2 mm diameter

Materials

Silver wire, 1.5 mm (16 swg) diameter, 300 mm
Silver wire, 0.8 mm (21 swg) diameter, about 300 mm
Hollow silver beads, 4 mm diameter (24) and 6 mm diameter (12)
Medium and easy silver solder
Bolt ring

Method

Cut the 1.5 mm wire into twelve equal lengths. Now thread one 6 mm bead on each link wire, flanked by two 4 mm beads. With medium solder, solder the assembly. Wind the 0.8 mm silver wire on the 2 mm rod and cut through into jump rings. Twist the jump rings flat and, using easy solder, solder one to each end of the bars. Three soldered jump rings are used to join the bars which gives the chain good flexibility. Pickle and polish the whole assembly.

Make and solder a 4 mm jump ring on one end of the chain and fit a bolt ring to the other end.

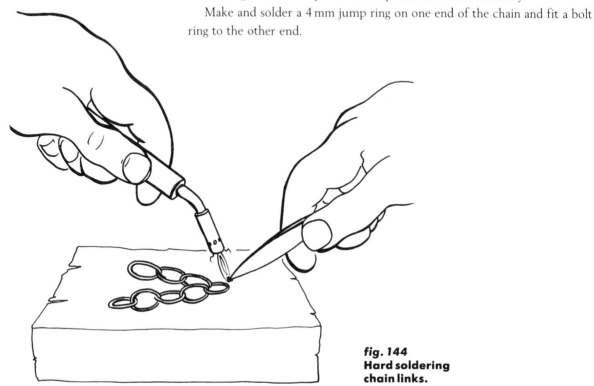

**fig. 144
Hard soldering
chain links.**

PROJECT 3

FANCY CHAIN

Tools and Equipment

Hard soldering equipment　　　　Polishing cloth

Material

Odd lengths of silver chain

Method

This chain is made from short lengths of various designs of chain. The pieces are joined by cutting through links and resoldering on the heavier chain, and by small suitably-sized jump rings for the finer chain.

The length and selection of chains depends on availability and required effect.

Although very simple in concept, the resulting unique chain can be most attractive.

**fig. 145
Fancy chain.**

16 Recovered and Found Materials

The great advantage of recovered and found materials is that they are free. This in no way detracts from the quality of the finished product.

The following are just some examples of recovered or found materials and their applications.

**fig. 146
Earrings cut from translucent green plastic bottle and decorated with enamel paint applied with a stamp cut from an eraser.**

Item	Application
Plastic containers, flexible and rigid	Plastic sheet for fabrication, vacuum-forming and hot-forming
Electrical wire insulation	Covering spring steel wire, making beads and short tubes
Food cans	Sheet in tin-plated steel or aluminium
Cutlery forks	Bangles
Cotton buds	Removing the ends makes a length of coloured plastic tube for beads etc.
Small animal skeletons	Bones, teeth and claws for decoration
Newspaper	For making papier-mâché
Colour magazine pages	Rolled paper beads
Plastic drinking straws	Beads and rods for earrings
Seeds, husks and nut shells	Threading as beads
Sea shells	Use complete as beads, or cut (pages 91–5)
Twigs and small branches	Natural wood beads and, when angle-cut, plaques
Out of circulation coins	As pendants or brooches. The background can be cut away.
Broken ceramics	Cut and mounted as pendants

Earrings made from coloured children's erasers (left) and from cut lengths of the plastic tubular centres of cotton buds (right). Just two examples of using recovered and found materials.

fig. 147
Necklace made from discs cut from a squeezy bottle, handpainted and spaced on wire links with cut lengths of electrical insulation sleeve.

fig. 148
Cut tin can pierced with
nails which were filed to
create shaped holes. The
piece is edged with copper
wire soft soldered in place.
A brooch pin is soldered to
the back.

fig. 149
Bracelet formed
from an old
fork.

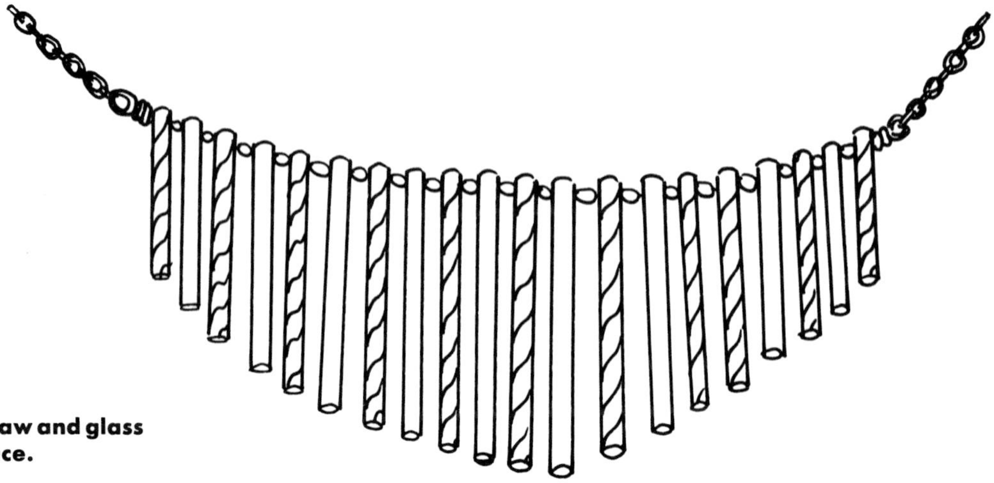

fig. 150
Drinking straw and glass
bead necklace.

Conversion Tables and General Information

METRIC/IMPERIAL CONVERSION TABLES

Millimetres	Inches
1	0.03937
2	0.07874
3	0.11811
4	0.15748
5	0.19685
6	0.23622
7	0.27559
8	0.31496
9	0.35433
10	0.3937

To convert millimetres to inches multiply by 0.03937

Centimetres	Inches
1	0.394
2	0.787
3	1.181
4	1.575
5	1.969
6	2.362
7	2.756
8	3.150
9	3.543
10	3.937

To convert centimetres to inches multiply by 0.394

Grammes	Ounces
1	0.0322
2	0.0643
3	0.0965
4	0.1286
5	0.1607
6	0.1929
7	0.2251
8	0.2572
9	0.2894
10	0.3215

To convert grammes to Troy ounces multiply by 0.03215

Temperatures

To convert Centigrade to Farenheit multiply by 9, divide by 5 and add 32.

METAL GAUGES FOR WIRE AND SHEET

Round wire and sheet metal is measured in a variety of ways. As well as inches and millimetres different industries and different countries use gauge numbers to specify thickness and diameter of sheet and wire. Commonly used gauges are shown in the tables.

BRITISH IMPERIAL STANDARD FOR WIRE AND SHEET WIRE GAUGE (SWG) INCHES AND MILLIMETRES

SWG No	Diameter in	mm
13	0.092	2.340
14	0.080	2.030
15	0.072	1.830
16	0.064	1.630
17	0.056	1.420
18	0.048	1.220
19	0.040	1.016
20	0.036	0.914
21	0.032	0.813
22	0.028	0.711
23	0.024	0.610
24	0.022	0.559
25	0.020	0.508
26	0.018	0.457
27	0.016	0.417
28	0.014	0.376
29	0.013	0.345
30	0.012	0.315
31	0.011	0.295

BIRMINGHAM METAL FOR WIRE AND SHEET GAUGE BRITISH INCHES AND MILLIMETRES

Gauge Number	Dimensions in	mm
10	0.1250	3.175
11	0.1113	2.827
12	0.0991	2.517
13	0.0882	2.24
14	0.0785	1.994
15	0.0699	1.775
16	0.0625	1.587
17	0.0556	1.412
18	0.0495	1.257
19	0.0440	1.118
20	0.0392	0.996
21	0.0349	0.886
22	0.0312	0.794
23	0.0278	0.707
24	0.0248	0.629
25	0.0220	0.560
26	0.0196	0.498
27	0.0174	0.4432
28	0.0156	0.3969
29	0.0139	0.3531
30	0.0123	0.3124

AMERICAN WIRE GAUGE STANDARDS
INCHES

Number of Wire Gauge	American or Brown & Sharpe	Stubs Steel Wire	U.S. Standard Gauge for Sheet and Plate Iron and Steel
8	0.1284	0.197	0.1718
9	0.1144	0.194	0.1562
10	0.1018	0.191	0.1406
11	0.0907	0.188	0.1250
12	0.0808	0.185	0.1093
13	0.0719	0.182	0.0937
14	0.0640	0.180	0.0781
15	0.0570	0.178	0.0703
16	0.0508	0.175	0.0625
17	0.0452	0.172	0.0562
18	0.0403	0.168	0.0500
19	0.0358	0.164	0.0437
20	0.0319	0.161	0.0375
21	0.0284	0.157	0.0343
22	0.0253	0.155	0.0312
23	0.0225	0.153	0.0281
24	0.0201	0.151	0.0250
25	0.0179	0.148	0.0218
26	0.0159	0.146	0.0187
27	0.0141	0.143	0.0171
28	0.0126	0.139	0.0156
29	0.0112	0.134	0.0140
30	0.0100	0.127	0.0125

PIERCING SAW: SIZES AND APPLICATIONS

Blade reference number	Thickness in inches	Width in inches	Teeth per inch	Suitable for material thickness:
M4/0	0.006	0.018	80	up to
M3/0	0.007	0.019	80	0.015 in
M2/0	0.008	0.021	60	0.016 in to
M1/0	0.009	0.023	60	0.030 in
M0	0.010	0.025	60	
M1	0.011	0.026	52	0.031 in to 0.45 in
M2	0.012	0.027	44	0.016 in to
M3	0.014	0.030	44	0.060 in
M4	0.015	0.032	32	0.061 in to 0.092 in
M5	0.017	0.036	32	over 0.061 in

Melting points for silver

Fine silver: 960°C (1760°F)
Standard or sterling silver: 893°C (1640°F)

Composition of typical silver solders

	Silver	Copper	Zinc
Easy	60	25	15
Medium	70	20	10
Hard	75	22	3

Etching acid for silver

3 parts water, 1 part nitric acid by volume
(Always add acid to water and store in a glass-stoppered glass bottle in a secure place.)

Gramme weights

1 gramme	= 15.43 grains troy
1 penny weight (dwt)	= 1.55 grammes
1 ounce troy	= 31.104 grammes
1 ounce avoirdupois	= 28.35 grammes

To convert troy ounces to avoirdupois, multiply by 1.09714
To convert avoirdupois ounces to troy, multiply by 0.91146
Karat weights (for stones)
1 karat=0.2 grammes

Dimensional guidelines

Choker	350 mm to 380 mm	(14 in to 15 in)
Short chain	406 mm	(16 in)
Medium chain	460 mm	(18 in)
Long chain	560 mm	(22 in)
Opening bracelets	165 mm inside circumference	(6½ in)
Bangles	66 mm inside diameter	(2 9/16 in)
	208 mm inside circumference	(8 3/16 in)
Ear wires (straight)	9.5 mm to 12.5 mm	(3/8 in to ½ in) long

Rings
Most popular sizes:

UK size	J	K	L	M	N	O	P
Inside diameter							
(in)	0.6145	0.63	0.646	0.661	0.677	0.692	0.708
(mm)	15.6	16	16.4	16.8	17.2	17.6	18
USA size	5	5½	6	6½	7	7½	8
Inside diameter							
(in)	0.614	0.630	0.650	0.662	0.678	0.694	0.710

STONES AND THEIR ASSOCIATIONS

Birth stones

January	garnet
February	amethyst
March	jasper, bloodstone, aquamarine
April	diamond, rock crystal
May	emerald, chrysoprase
June	pearl, moonstone
July	ruby, carnelian
August	peridot, sardonyx, jade
September	sapphire, lapis lazuli, coral
October	opal, tourmaline
November	topaz, amber, citrine
December	turquoise

Wedding anniversaries

Year	stone/metal	Year	stone/metal
1	aquamarine	13	agate
2	crystal	14	ivory
3	chrysoprase	15	topaz
4	moonstone	25	silver
5	carnelian	30	pearl
6	peridot	35	jade
7	coral	40	ruby
8	opal	45	sapphire
9	citrine	50	gold
10	turquoise	55	emerald
11	garnet	60	diamond
12	amethyst		

Glossary

alloy: a metal comprising two or more metals

annealing: the heat treatment of a metal. To relieve work-hardened metals and return them to a soft condition

anodizing: a protective, sometimes coloured, finish used on aluminium alloy items

assay: the testing of precious metals to determine the composition

baguette: the rectangular shape of a precious stone

baroque pearl: an unsymmetrical natural pearl

base metal: any non-precious metal

bench pin/peg: a hardwood or plywood block with a 'V' shape cut out of it. It is fitted to a jeweller's bench and used for supporting the piece being worked on

bezel: the rim or hoop of metal used to contain a stone or similar element

binding wire: iron wire used to hold parts together during soldering

broach: a tapered tool with cutting edges for enlarging holes

burnisher: a hand-held tool with a polished metal or stone tip set in a wooden handle – used for burnishing metal smooth and forming over a bezel

burr: a small drill-like cutting tool, sometimes called a Fraiser, which cuts on its diameter rather than its end; burr also refers to a sharp raised edge on cut metal

cabochon: the cut of a dome-shaped stone

capillary action: the physical phenomenon whereby a liquid is drawn into a narrow gap

champlevé: a form of enamelling in which enamel is fired into etched or cut recesses in metal

chasing: punched decoration in sheet metal done from the front of a piece

collet: the metal support for a stone

crimps: small diameter tubes in short lengths which can be threaded over two components and then crimped to secure

cut-out: either the piece cut from or the hole left in a metal sheet piece

dapping block (also doming block): a metal block with hemispherical indentations of various diameters

die: a metal block in which a hole or pattern has been cut and into or through which metal is forced to create a pattern or shape

drawing: pulling wire or other sections sequentially through a series of holes to change and reduce the shape

electrum: an alloy of gold and silver

engineer's blue: a blue lacquer for coating metal through which lines are scribed when marking out

facet: a flat face, as on a gem stone

ferrous metal: any metal containing iron

filigree: a framed form of decoration made with various sections and twists of silver wire

findings: all the small commonly used parts incorporated into jewellery

fire stain: a dark grey layer of copper oxide brought to the surface of silver when it is heated

flux: a chemical in powder or liquid form used during soldering to prevent the formation of oxides which inhibit the process

forging: changing the shape of metal with hammer blows

fusing: bringing metal to the near liquid state so that it will join on contact

granulation: surface decoration by very small spheres in patterns

hallmark: the mark struck by an assay office indicating the quality of metal, the maker and where and when it was assayed

hard solder: solder with a melting range of between $667°C$ and $800°C$. A gas torch is needed for soldering at these temperatures

ingot: a cast bar of metal

intaglio: a design carved into the surface of a material

jump ring: a small ring of metal used for suspending or joining parts

lemel: fine scrap precious metal produced by filing

mandrel: a cylindrical rod, often tapered, around which pieces are shaped

Marquise: an oval shape pointed at the ends, used in the description of stones

millefiori: Italian for 'thousand flowers', refers to small bunches of coloured glass cane, arranged so that end view resembles a flower. It is available cut into short lengths

muratic acid: hydrochloric acid

mokume: a Japanese name for the surface decoration simulating wood grain

nickel silver: sometimes called German silver, it is an alloy of copper, nickel and zinc but contains no silver

niello: a mixture essentially of silver, copper, lead and sulphur used for filling shallow cavities and producing a darker surface decoration on silver

oxidize: surface colour change to metals when oxygen combines with metal, for example when the metal is heated and cools in air

paillon: a small snippet of solder

pectoral: a chest decoration

pickle: a solution used to remove oxides and flux

piercing: cutting shapes in sheet metal with a jeweller's saw

pitch bowl: a heavy cast metal bowl of hemispherical shape filled with a pitch-based mixture – used to support sheet metal pieces when being worked with punches

pinchbeck: an imitation of gold made from an alloy of copper and zinc

quenching: rapid cooling of hot metal by sudden immersion in liquid, usually water

repoussé: relief shape punched from the back

riffler: a fine file with upturned end used for reaching below a surface

rouge: fine polishing compound

scratch brush: stiff wire brush used to create a multiple scratch finish on a surface

snips: short-bladed, scissor-like tool for cutting sheet metal – both straight and curved blades are available

solder: a metal alloy with a melting point less than that of the metals to be joined

sprue: the piece in a casting joining the metal supply to the body of the piece

swage block: metal block, generally steel, cut with a graduated range of semi-circular grooves – used for forming flat sheet metal

Swiss file: small files with integral handles, available in a range of cross-sections and grades of cut

tempering: slightly reducing a dead hard piece of steel to make it more springy

tinning: flowing a thin surface of solder on a metal face

triblet: a tapered length of steel used for shaping rings and bracelets

tripoli: a coarse abrasive

water of Ayr stone (also Scotch stone): a soft slate-like material available in sticks and used wet for rubbing away precious metals

work-hardening: hardening of metal by repeated deformation like hammering, twisting or drawing

Bibliography

Abbey, S., *The Goldsmiths' and Silversmiths' Handbook* (London, Technical Press, 1952, revised edn 1968)

Arem, J., *Gems* (London, Bantam Books, 1975)

Bagley, P., *Making Silver Jewellery* (London, Batsford, 1982)

Blakemore, K., *Management for the Retail Jeweller* (London, Iliffe Books)

British Museum, *Jewellery through 7000 Years* (London, Trustees of the British Museum, 1976)

Divis, J., *Silver Marks of the World* (London, Hamlyn, 1976)

Edwards, R., *The Techniques of Jewellery* (London, Batsford, 1977)

Emerson, A. R., *Handmade Jewellery* (England, Dryad Press, 1953)

Geer, G., *The Silversmiths' Handbook* (London, Crosby Lockwood & Son, 1885)

Goodden, R. and Popham, P., *Silversmithing* (Oxford University Press, 1971)

Graham-Campbell, J. and Kidd, D., *The Vikings* (London, Trustees of the British Museum, 1980)

Harries, J., *Your Business and the Law* (London, Oyez Publishing, 1975)

Higgins, R., *Jewellery from Classical Lands* (London, Trustees of the British Museum, 1976)

Mourney, G., *Art Nouveau Jewellery and Fans* (Dover, 1973)

Neumann, R., von, *The Design and Creation of Jewellery* (London, Isaac Pitman & Son Ltd, 1962)

Shoenfelt, J., *Designing and Making Handwrought Jewellery* (New York, McGraw-Hill, 1960).

Taylor, G. and Scarisbrick, D., *Finger Rings from Ancient Egypt to the Present Day* (London, Lund Humphries Ltd)

Untracht, O., *Metal Techniques for Craftsmen* (London, Robert Hale, 1969)

Index